General Instructions

You probably already have most of the supplies needed for these projects. Even so, here are a few tips on materials and tools, and general assembly instructions and finishing that you may find helpful.

Supplies

Here is a list of recommended supplies you will need to make the pot holders. Review the list of supplies to make sure you have what you need before you begin.

- Large variety of scrap cotton fabrics, including WOF strips
- Cotton backing fabric approximately 10" square for each pot holder
- Scrap cotton batting approximately 10" square for each pot holder
- Heat-resistant batting approximately 10" square for each pot holder
- Fusible web with paper release if using the appliqué options
- Cotton thread
- Rotary cutter and mat
- Scissors for paper and fabric
- Nonslip quilting rulers
- Water-soluble marker
- Straight pins
- Hand-sewing needles
- Seam ripper
- Iron and ironing surface
- Sewing machine in good working order
- Sewing machine needles: Microtec 70/10 are recommended

Skill Level

The skill level for all the projects in this book is beginner but don't let that stop you if you're a more skilled quilter. Any quilter can benefit from this diverse collection of 8½" blocks.

This collection of pot holders is perfect for skill building, and the variety of 8½" unfinished blocks can be further used to design your own quilt projects. Don't stop with making the pot holders—continue on and work your favorite blocks into table runners, wall hangings, quilts or whatever way your inspiration takes you!

Battings

When making pot holders it's a good idea to use a heat-resistant batting to prevent injury and protect surfaces. I recommend Poly-Therm heat-resistant fleece by Bosal. It's lightweight, easy to quilt through, washes like a dream and is very reasonable in cost. However, there are several brands on the market; the important thing is to use a heat-resistant batting. Be sure to read the manufacturer's instructions before beginning since there are some differences between products from different manufacturers.

As an extra precaution, it is recommended to use a layer of cotton batting in addition to heat-resistant batting when making pot holders. Think of it as a great way to use up all those small pieces of batting that have been accumulating in your sewing room! It's also recommended to use cotton thread since polyester or blended threads may not hold up to heat.

Also note that heat-resistant batting is not microwave safe. If you want something you can place in the microwave, use several layers of cotton batting instead.

To sum up: For the best results and the safest pot holder place one layer each of cotton batting and heat-resistant batting in between the pieced block and the backing fabric before quilting the layers together with cotton thread.

Block Construction

Every block in this book will finish to an 8" block if sewn into a larger project. If you are making pot holders, they will finish to 8½" because the binding covers the edges that would be the seam allowance in another type of project.

All piecing is sewn right sides together with ¼" seams and should be pressed after each step.

Read all the instructions before beginning each block.

The following abbreviations are used in the instructions:

WOF – width of fabric

HST – half square triangle ◻

QST – quarter square triangle ◻

Cut out all the pieces before you begin, to make sure you have enough fabric to complete the block. Some cutting instructions for HST and QST will result in more pieces than required. Simply set aside these extra pieces for another project (or for additional pot holders!).

For a smooth and crisp finish, press all seams again before adding the battings and backing. When working with triangles cut on the bias, it is sometimes helpful to iron triangles with spray starch before assembly to prevent stretching. To complete a pot holder, first make the block. Once you have completed the piecing for the block, press all seams flat. Then, on a flat surface, make a "sandwich" by stacking the backing fabric right side down, the heat-resistant batting, the cotton batting and then the block right side up. It makes a difference with some heat-resistant battings which side is up or down, so read the manufacturer's instructions. The side with the heat-resistant batting is meant to be against hot items, so if you are making hot pads for the table rather than pot holders, place the heat-resistant batting on top of the cotton batting as it reflects heat back to the source. Next, smooth out and pin-baste the four layers together. Quilt as desired and then bind.

Binding

To make the binding for your pot holder begin with a coordinating-fabric 2½" x WOF strip.

Press the strip in half lengthwise with wrong sides together.

Starting at one corner of the pot holder with raw edges even, stitch the folded strip to the block side using a ¼" seam allowance. Stop ¼" from the first corner as shown in Figure 1a and pivot to stitch off the sandwich. Rotate the pot holder to the left and fold the strip up to make a 45-degree angle as shown in Figure 1b. Referring to Figure 1c, fold the binding back down to match the raw edge of the sandwich and stitch the same as the first side. Continue on each side until you reach the last side.

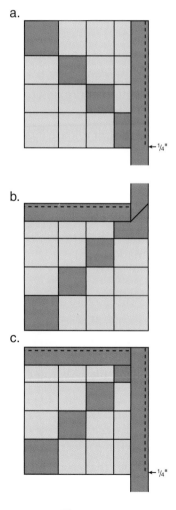

Figure 1

Before stitching the last side, turn the starting section of the binding over to the back side of the potholder, in the same manner as it would be turned to finish on the back, and pin to secure as shown in Figure 2.

Figure 2

Referring to Figure 3, stitch the last side straight on, backstitching at the edge of the sandwich to secure. Cut the strip, leaving a 6" tail for making the loop.

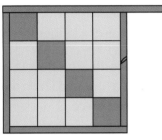

Figure 3

Turn the binding to the back and slip-stitch into place all the way around and stopping at the tail. Fold and press the tail so that all the raw edges are inside and the width of the tail matches the width of the binding.

Return to your sewing machine and stitch from the inner edge of the vertical binding to the end of the tail with a straight stitch as shown in Figure 4.

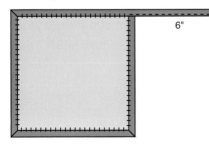

Figure 4

Referring to Figure 5, bring the end of the tail around to the front of the pot holder and place over the binding so that it matches and lines up with it. Use a zigzag stitch to secure the end.

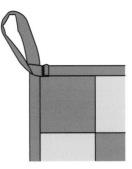

Figure 5

If you choose to make hot pads instead, bind as you would for any quilt. Hot pads are intended to use as a table or surface protection and do not require a loop as a finish.

Options

As always, I think there should be options to any project, even pot holders. Quilters should feel free to add their own personal touches and personality to each and every project they make. Therefore, I've taken a few of the pot holders, added my ideas to them and am sharing them with you. By all means don't think this is the only way to finish these pot holders. If you have an idea, please do run with it! I only hope that these few ideas will inspire you to be creative with your pot holders and maybe personalize some of them for gifts.

This section offers you a few creative options for your pot holders. There are many ways to add elements to them and you are only as limited as your imagination. Some of the examples in the book involve appliqué, fussy cutting and writing words with free-motion quilting. If you think of another finish for your pot holders, by all means do experiment!

Fusible Appliqué

All the appliqué designs given are reversed for fusible applique. If you're going to use another appliqué technique you may need to reverse the drawings and add seam allowances.

After selecting the appliqué you will be using, trace the shape(s) onto the paper side of fusible web. Leave at least a ¼" between the shapes. I use Bosal Splendid Web fusible because it is lightweight and very reliable. Be sure to read the manufacturer's instructions for the fusible web you choose to use.

Once you have traced your shapes on the paper side of the fusible web, place the fusible web paper side up on the wrong side of the fabric and press. Once the the web/fabric is cool, cut out the individual shapes on the drawn lines. Arrange the pieces on the block in numerical order referring to the chosen appliqué pattern. If using the suggested appliqués given, the layout should be easy to follow. Once you have the pieces arranged and are satisfied with it, press into place.

Fusible Woven Stabilizer

Another consideration before you stitch your appliqué into place is whether to use a fusible woven stabilizer. I use Bosal Fashion Fuse #300. Read the manufacturer's instructions before applying a stabilizer if you choose to add it to your block. A stabilizer is applied to the wrong side of the block and ensures that the fabric will lay nice and flat as the stitching is added, resulting in a better-looking block. It is not required, but I do recommend it. After you have applied the stabilizer, use your chosen appliqué stitch to stitch the appliqué in place.

Tips for Machine-Stitched Fusible Appliqué Success

Reduce your machine's stitch length to 1.9 or 2.0. The smaller the stitch length the easier it will be to stitch around the appliqué shape with ease, and you won't get that choppy look of a longer stitch.

Use a Microtec 70/10 needle. This needle will piece through the fabrics with a nice small hole and look much nicer for the finished piece.

Always pull the bobbin thread to the top. This will prevent the dreaded "thread nest" on the back of the piece you're appliquéing.

Always stop in the needle-down position. That way, if you have to adjust the direction, which you will have to do often with this type of appliqué, you won't lose your stitch spacing. Just remember that every time you stop, make sure the needle is down.

Go slowly. A nice slow speed will help keep your stitches nice and neat and will allow you to make any adjustments to the direction. Keep your stitches as even as possible for a uniform finish. You'll be glad you did!

Raw-Edge Fusible Appliqué

One of the easiest ways to appliqué is the fusible-web method. Paper-backed fusible web motifs are fused to the wrong side of fabric, cut out and then fused to a foundation fabric and stitched in place by hand or machine. You can use this method for raw- or turned-edge appliqué.

1. If the appliqué motif is directional, it should be reversed for raw-edge fusible appliqué. If doing several identical appliqué motifs, trace reverse motif shapes onto template material to make reusable templates.

2. Use templates or trace the appliqué motif shapes onto paper side of paper-backed fusible web. Leave at least ½" between shapes. Cut out shapes leaving a margin around traced lines.

3. Follow manufacturer's instructions and fuse shapes to wrong side of fabric as indicated on pattern for color and number to cut.

4. Cut out appliqué shapes on traced lines and remove paper backing from fusible web. *Note: If doing turned-edge applique, cut out applique ⅛" outside the traced lines. Then fold edges to wrong side on traced lines.*

5. Again following manufacturer's instructions, arrange and fuse pieces on the foundation fabric referring to appliqué motif included in pattern.

6. Hand- or machine-stitch around edges. *Note: Position a light- to mediumweight stabilizer behind the appliqué motif to keep the fabric from puckering during machine stitching. Some stitch possibilities include machine- or hand-satin or zigzag, buttonhole or blanket and running stitch.*

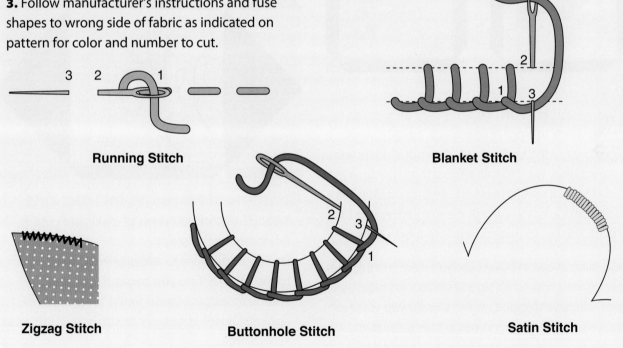

Running Stitch

Blanket Stitch

Zigzag Stitch

Buttonhole Stitch

Satin Stitch

Fussy Cutting

Another way to be creative with your pot holders is to add a special fabric to the center piece of the block. There are several blocks in this book that will allow you to add a fussy-cut motif to them. Some of the examples are Week No. 40 and Week No. 49. To fussy-cut a motif, first you must find a fabric motif that fits inside the seam lines of the piece. In the example given, the center piece is a 4½" square. With

a clear quilting ruler it was easy to see and to center the motifs to fit into the 4½" square. Once you have centered the motif, simply cut out the square in the size needed.

Words or Messages in Free-Motion Quilting

Adding words to a pot holder block is a special way to personalize it. If you're gifting the pot holders you make you may want to think about this technique as a way to add a special message. Adding words takes a bit of practice, but it is worth the extra effort you take to do it. The key to success here is to have a plan.

First, think about the message you want to add. The space is very limited on an 8½" unfinished block. Once you have decided on the word(s) you want to add, practice writing it on paper that is cut to the same size as the space you have available on the block. If it's a 4" finished square of fabric, practice writing the message on a 4" square of paper. Once you're comfortable with the size of the writing and the space, you're ready to begin.

Next, use a water-soluble marker to write the word or message on the pot holder where you want it to be. Once you are satisfied with how it looks in the allotted space, pin the layers of your pot holder together and you're ready to give it a go.

Figure out your quilting path before you begin. Go nice and slow and, if need be, stitch over the same writing a couple of times. That's what I do to make it show up darker and better. Once you are comfortable with your progress, begin to stitch the words slowly onto the pot holder sandwich following the water-soluble writing. It is much easier to quilt in cursive than printed letters because of the stops and starts. Also, dot your i's and cross your t's after you've finished the continuous quilting. You may have to go over the writing a few times to make it dark enough to read well at a distance. If you can't be exact that's fine. It will look just fine if all the lines are close to each other.

Condensed Finishing Instructions

- Select the block you want to make and cotton fabrics from your stash.
- Decide if you want to add any extra finishing to the block before you begin. If you are adding an extra element to the block, such as appliqué, fussy-cut pieces or stitched words, plan accordingly.
- Cut the pieces out and stitch the block together using cotton thread.
- Press all the seams flat.
- Add appliqué or write a word or message with a water-soluble pen if you so desire.

- To make the quilt "sandwich," layer on a flat surface bottom to top as follows: backing fabric right side down, heat-resistant batting, cotton batting and the pieced block right side up.

- Pin-baste sandwich and quilt as desired.
- Follow the binding instructions given to add the binding and make the loop.
- Enjoy! And of course, you'll want to start another! ●

Fussy Cutting

The quilting term "fussy-cut" refers to selectively cutting fabric to create patch or unit shapes that showcase a particular motif or part of the fabric pattern.

1. Make a fussy-cutting template from a piece of cardstock, cardboard or frosted plastic template material 2" larger all around than the size of the finished fussy-cut shape desired. For example, if the fussy-cut finished piece will be 4" square, you will need a piece of template material at least 6" square.

2. Draw the size of the finished fussy-cut shape onto the template material, then add a 1" border all the way around (Photo A).

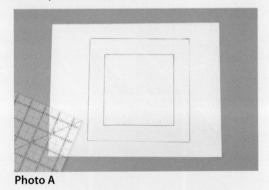

Photo A

3. Cut out the center fussy-cut shape so you have a viewing-window template the finished size of the patch/unit needed (Photo B).

Photo B

4. Use this window to audition areas of the fabric to make sure they will fit within the finished shape size and not disappear into the seams (Photo C).

Photo C

5. When you are happy with the fabric motif in the viewing window area, use a water-soluble marker to trace around the inside of the window (Photo D).

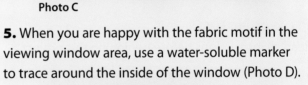

Photo D

6. Add a ¼" seam allowance around the traced area and cut out the shape.

Week No. 1

Anvil

Finished Size

Pot Holder Size:
8½" x 8½"

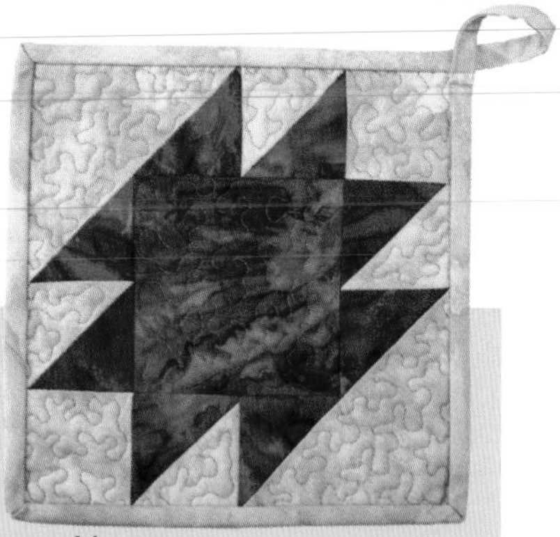

Materials

- 1 (2½" x WOF) coordinating fabric for binding and loop
- Scrap light fabric
- Scrap dark fabric
- 10" x 10" backing
- 10" x 10" heat-resistant batting
- 10" x 10" cotton batting
- Thread
- Basic sewing tools and supplies

Project Notes

Read all instructions before beginning this project.

Stitch right sides together using a ¼" seam allowance unless otherwise specified.

Materials and cutting lists assume 40" of usable fabric width for yardage.

WOF – width of fabric
HST – half square triangle ⧅
QST – quarter square triangle ⊠

Cutting

From light fabric cut:

- 1 (4⅞") A square then cut once diagonally ⧅
- 2 (2⅞") B squares then cut once diagonally ⧅
- 2 (2½") C squares

From dark fabric cut:

- 1 (4½") D square
- 4 (2⅞") E squares then cut once diagonally ⧅

Completing the Block

1. Stitch one B HST and one E HST together as shown in Figure 1. Press open. Make 4.

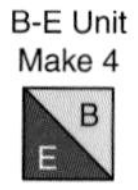

Figure 1

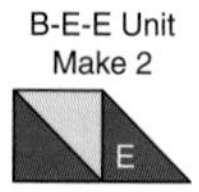

Figure 2

2. Stitch one unit from step 1 and one E HST as shown in Figure 2. Press. Make 2.

3. Stitch one C square and one E HST to each side of a unit from step 1 as shown in Figure 3. Press. Make 2.

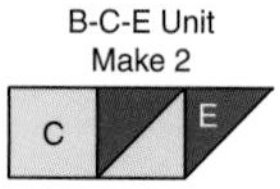

Figure 3

4. Referring to the Assembly Diagram and photo, lay out all pieces and units as shown and stitch together to complete one block. Press.

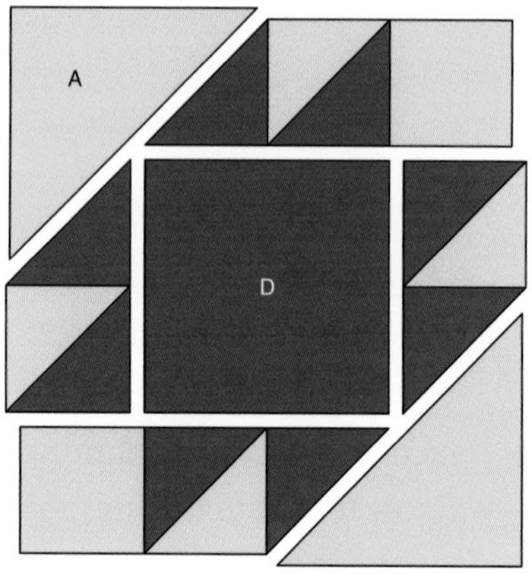

Week No. 1: Anvil
Assembly Diagram 8½" x 8½"

5. Layer backing right side down, battings and pot holder block right side up. Quilt as desired. Bind pot holder and make hanging loop referring to General Instructions on page 3.

Devil's Claw

Finished Size

Pot Holder Size:
8½" x 8½"

Materials

- 1 (2½" x WOF)
  coordinating
  fabric for binding and loop
- Scrap light fabric
- Scrap dark fabric
- 10" x 10" backing
- 10" x 10" heat-resistant batting
- 10" x 10" cotton batting
- Thread
- Basic sewing tools and supplies

Project Notes

Read all instructions before beginning this project.

Stitch right sides together using a ¼" seam allowance unless otherwise specified.

Materials and cutting lists assume 40" of usable fabric width for yardage.

WOF – width of fabric
HST – half square triangle ◺
QST – quarter square triangle ⊠

Cutting

From light fabric cut:

- 3 (5¼") A squares then cut twice diagonally ⊠
- 2 (2⅞") B squares then cut once diagonally ◺

From dark fabric cut:

- 3 (5¼") C squares then cut twice diagonally ⊠
- 2 (2⅞") D squares then cut once diagonally ◺

Completing the Block

1. Stitch one C QST and one A QST together as shown in Figure 1a. Press. Make 2. Stitch the two units together as shown in Figure 1b. Press.

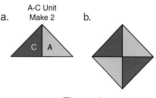

a. A-C Unit
    Make 2

b.

Figure 1

2. Stitch one D HST to each side of an A QST as shown in Figure 2. Press. Make 2.

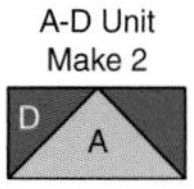

A-D Unit
Make 2

Figure 2

A-C-C Unit
Make 2

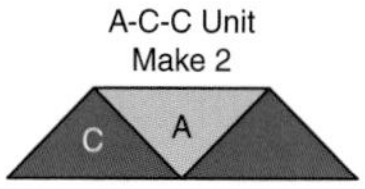

Figure 3

3. Stitch one C QST to each side of an A QST as shown in Figure 3. Press. Make 2.

4. Stitch a B HST to each end of the unit from step 3 as shown in Figure 4. Press. Make 2.

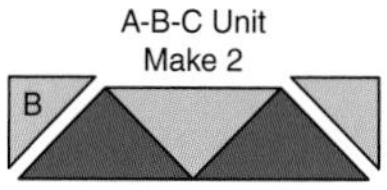

A-B-C Unit
Make 2

Figure 4

5. Referring to the photo and Assembly Diagram, lay out all units as shown and stitch together to complete one block. Press.

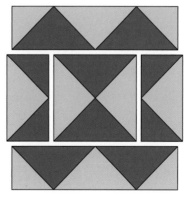

Week No. 2: Devil's Claw
Assembly Diagram 8½" x 8½"

6. Layer backing right side down, battings and pot holder block right side up. Quilt as desired. Bind pot holder and make hanging loop referring to General Instructions on page 3. ●

In Flight

Finished Size

Pot Holder Size:
8½" x 8½"

Materials

- 1 (2½" x WOF) coordinating fabric for binding and loop
- Scrap light fabric
- Scrap medium fabric
- Scrap dark fabric
- 10" x 10" backing
- 10" x 10" heat-resistant batting
- 10" x 10" cotton batting
- Thread
- Basic sewing tools and supplies

Project Notes

Read all instructions before beginning this project.

Stitch right sides together using a ¼" seam allowance unless otherwise specified.

Materials and cutting lists assume 40" of usable fabric width for yardage.

WOF – width of fabric
HST – half square triangle
QST – quarter square triangle

Cutting

From light fabric cut:

- 1 (4⅞") A square then cut once diagonally
- 5 (2⅞") B squares then cut once diagonally

From medium fabric cut:

- 2 (4⅞") C squares then cut once diagonally

From dark fabric cut:

- 2 (2⅞") D squares then cut once diagonally

Completing the Block

1. Stitch one B HST and one D HST together as shown in Figure 1. Press. Make 3.

B-D Unit
Make 3

B-D Triangle Unit
Make 3

Figure 1　　　　**Figure 2**

2. Stitch one B HST to the side and then bottom of the unit from step 1 as shown in Figure 2. Press. Make 3.

3. Stitch one C HST to each of the units from step 2 as shown in Figure 3. Press. Make 3.

Quarter Block Unit
Make 3

A-C Unit
Make 1

Figure 3　　　　**Figure 4**

4. Stitch one A HST and one C HST together as shown in Figure 4. Press.

5. Referring to the photo and Assembly Diagram, lay out all units as shown and stitch together to complete one block. Press.

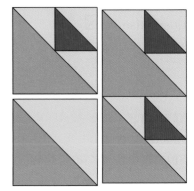

Week No. 3: In Flight
Assembly Diagram 8½" x 8½"

6. Layer backing right side down, battings and pot holder block right side up. Quilt as desired. Bind pot holder and make hanging loop referring to General Instructions on page 3. ●

Cypress

Finished Size

Pot Holder Size:
8½" x 8½"

Materials

- 1 (2½" x WOF) coordinating fabric for binding and loop
- Scrap light fabric
- Scrap medium fabric
- Scrap dark fabric
- 10" x 10" backing
- 10" x 10" heat-resistant batting
- 10" x 10" cotton batting
- Thread
- Basic sewing tools and supplies

Project Notes

Read all instructions before beginning this project.

Stitch right sides together using a ¼" seam allowance unless otherwise specified.

Materials and cutting lists assume 40" of usable fabric width for yardage.

WOF – width of fabric
HST – half square triangle ◻
QST – quarter square triangle ⊠

Cutting

From light fabric cut:

- 1 (4½") A square
- 6 (2⅞") B squares then cut once diagonally ◻

From medium fabric cut:

- 2 (2⅞") C squares then cut once diagonally ◻

From dark fabric cut:

- 1 (5¼") D square then cut twice diagonally ⊠

Completing the Block

1. Stitch one B HST and one C HST together as shown in Figure 1. Press. Make 4.

B-C Unit
Make 4

Figure 1

2. Stitch one B HST to each side of a D QST as shown in Figure 2. Press. Make 4.

B-D Unit
Make 4

Figure 2

3. Stitch one unit from step 1 to each end of a unit from step 2 as shown in Figure 3. Press. Make 2.

B-C-D Unit
Make 2

Figure 3

4. Referring to the photo and Assembly Diagram, lay out all units and the A square as shown and stitch together to complete one block. Press.

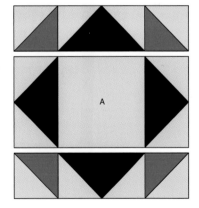

Week No. 4: Cypress
Assembly Diagram 8½" x 8½"

5. Layer backing right side down, battings and pot holder block right side up. Quilt as desired. Bind pot holder and make hanging loop referring to General Instructions on page 3.

Optional Center Square Finish

This is a great block to add a personalized option to. You can add an appliqué to the middle square or stitch in a meaningful word, saying or message. In the example given for this block the words "let's eat" were free-motion machine-quilted on the center square of the pot holder. To add your personal message, after the block is pieced, simply use a water-soluble marking pen to write a word or message. Then, when quilting the block, slowly free-motion machine-quilt over the markings. Once the quilting and binding are complete, follow the manufacturer's instructions to remove the markings. ●

Week No. 4 Option: Let's Eat
Placement Diagram 8½" x 8½"

Doubles

Finished Size
Pot Holder Size:
8½" x 8½"

Materials
- 1 (2½" x WOF)
  coordinating
  fabric for binding and loop
- Scrap light fabric
- Scrap dark fabric
- 10" x 10" backing
- 10" x 10" heat-resistant batting
- 10" x 10" cotton batting
- Thread
- Basic sewing tools and supplies

Project Notes
Read all instructions before beginning this project.

Stitch right sides together using a ¼" seam allowance unless otherwise specified.

Materials and cutting lists assume 40" of usable fabric width for yardage.

WOF – width of fabric
HST – half square triangle ◹
QST – quarter square triangle ⊠

Cutting

From light fabric cut:
- 4 (2⅞") A squares then cut once diagonally ◹
- 4 (2½") B squares

From dark fabric cut:
- 1 (4⅞") C square then cut once diagonally ◹
- 2 (2⅞") D squares then cut once diagonally ◹
- 2 (2½") E squares

Completing the Block

1. Stitch one A HST and one D HST together as shown in Figure 1. Press. Make 4.

A-D Unit
Make 4

Figure 1

A-B-D Unit
Make 4

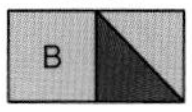

Figure 2

2. Stitch one B square to each unit from step 1 as shown in Figure 2. Press. Make 4.

3. Stitch two units from step 2 together as shown in Figure 3. Press. Make 2.

Quarter Block Unit
Make 2

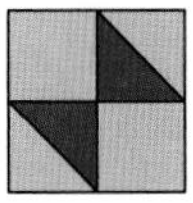

Figure 3

A-E Unit
Make 2

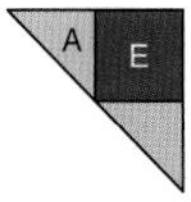

Figure 4

4. Stitch two A HST to one E square as shown in Figure 4. Press. Make 2.

5. Stitch one C HST to the unit from step 4 as shown in Figure 5. Press. Make 2.

A-C-E Unit
Make 2

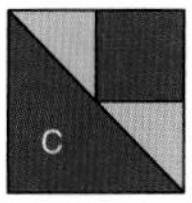

Figure 5

6. Referring to the photo and Assembly Diagram, lay out all units as shown and stitch together to complete one block. Press.

Week No. 5: Doubles
Assembly Diagram 8½" x 8½"

7. Layer backing right side down, battings and pot holder block right side up. Quilt as desired. Bind pot holder and make hanging loop referring to General Instructions on page 3. ●

Cross to Bear

Finished Size

Pot Holder Size:
8½" x 8½"

Materials

- 1 (2½" x WOF) coordinating fabric for binding and loop
- Scrap light fabric
- Scrap dark fabric
- 10" x 10" backing
- 10" x 10" heat-resistant batting
- 10" x 10" cotton batting
- Thread
- Basic sewing tools and supplies

Project Notes

Read all instructions before beginning this project.

Stitch right sides together using a ¼" seam allowance unless otherwise specified.

Materials and cutting lists assume 40" of usable fabric width for yardage.

WOF – width of fabric
HST – half square triangle ◹
QST – quarter square triangle ◩

Cutting

From light fabric cut:

- 4 (2½") A squares
- 1 (6⅛") B square

From dark fabric cut:

- 4 (2⅞") C squares then cut once diagonally ◹

Completing the Block

1. Stitch one C HST to two sides of one A square as shown in Figure 1. Press. Make 4.

A-C-C Unit
Make 4

A C

Figure 1

2. Referring to the photo and Assembly Diagram, lay out all units with B square as shown and stitch together to complete one block. Press.

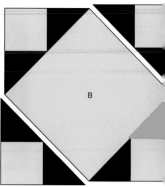

Week No. 6: Cross to Bear
Assembly Diagram 8½" x 8½"

3. Layer backing right side down, battings and pot holder block right side up. Quilt as desired. Bind pot holder and make hanging loop referring to General Instructions on page 3.

Optional Center Square Finish

This is a great block to add a personalized option to. You can add an appliqué to the middle square or stitch in a meaningful word, saying or message. In the example given for this block the words "Kiss the Cook" were free-motion machine-quilted on the center square of the pot holder. To add your personal message, after the block is pieced, simply use a water-soluble marking pen to write a word or message. Then, when quilting the block, slowly free-motion machine-quilt over the markings. Once the quilting and binding are complete, follow the manufacturer's instructions to remove the markings. ●

Week No. 6 Option: Kiss the Cook
Placement Diagram 8½" x 8½"

Bailey's Block

Finished Size

Pot Holder Size:
8½" x 8½"

Materials

- 1 (2½" x WOF) coordinating fabric for binding and loop
- Scrap light fabric
- Scrap medium fabric
- Scrap dark fabric
- 10" x 10" backing
- 10" x 10" heat-resistant batting
- 10" x 10" cotton batting
- Thread
- Basic sewing tools and supplies

Project Notes

Read all instructions before beginning this project.

Stitch right sides together using a ¼" seam allowance unless otherwise specified.

Materials and cutting lists assume 40" of usable fabric width for yardage.

WOF – width of fabric
HST – half square triangle
QST – quarter square triangle

Cutting

From light fabric cut:

- 2 (4½") A squares

From medium fabric cut:

- 1 (4⅞") B square then cut once diagonally

From dark fabric cut:

- 1 (4⅞") C square then cut once diagonally

Completing the Block

1. Stitch one B HST and one C HST together as shown in Figure 1. Press. Make 2.

B-C Unit
Make 2

Figure 1

2. Referring to the photo and Assembly Diagram, lay out all units as shown and stitch together to complete one block. Press.

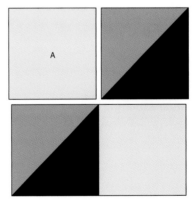

Week No. 7: Bailey's Block
Assembly Diagram 8½" x 8½"

3. Layer backing right side down, battings and pot holder block right side up. Quilt as desired. Bind pot holder and make hanging loop referring to General Instructions on page 3. ●

Yin Yang

Finished Size

Pot Holder Size:
8½" x 8½"

Materials

- 1 (2½" x WOF) coordinating fabric for binding and loop
- Scrap light fabric
- Scrap dark fabric
- 10" x 10" backing
- 10" x 10" heat-resistant batting
- 10" x 10" cotton batting
- Thread
- Basic sewing tools and supplies

Project Notes

Read all instructions before beginning this project.

Stitch right sides together using a ¼" seam allowance unless otherwise specified.

Materials and cutting lists assume 40" of usable fabric width for yardage.

WOF – width of fabric
HST – half square triangle
QST – quarter square triangle ⊠

Cutting

From light fabric cut:

- 2 (4⅞") A squares then cut once diagonally ◻
- 2 (2⅞") B squares then cut once diagonally ◻
- 4 (1½") C squares

From dark fabric cut:

- 4 (2⅞") D squares then cut once diagonally ◻
- 4 (1⅞") E squares then cut once diagonally ◻

Completing the Block

1. Stitch one E HST to the top and side of one C square as shown in Figure 1. Press. Make 4.

Figure 1 / **Figure 2**

2. Stitch one B HST to the unit from step 1 as shown in Figure 2. Press. Make 4.

3. Stitch one D HST to the top and side of the unit from step 2 as shown in Figure 3. Press. Make 4.

Figure 3 / **Figure 4**

4. Stitch one A triangle to each of the units from step 3 as shown in Figure 4. Press. Make 4.

5. Referring to the photo and Assembly Diagram, lay out all units as shown and stitch together to complete one block. Press.

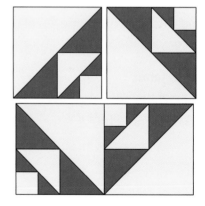

Week No. 8: Yin Yang
Assembly Diagram 8½" x 8½"

6. Layer backing right side down, battings and pot holder block right side up. Quilt as desired. Bind pot holder and make hanging loop referring to General Instructions on page 3. ●

Connecticut

Finished Size
Pot Holder Size:
8½" x 8½"

Materials
- 1 (2½" x WOF)
  coordinating
  fabric for binding and loop
- Scrap light fabric
- Scrap dark fabric
- 10" x 10" backing
- 10" x 10" heat-resistant batting
- 10" x 10" cotton batting
- Thread
- Basic sewing tools and supplies

Project Notes
Read all instructions before beginning this project.

Stitch right sides together using a ¼" seam allowance unless otherwise specified.

Materials and cutting lists assume 40" of usable fabric width for yardage.

WOF – width of fabric
HST – half square triangle ◻
QST – quarter square triangle ◻

Cutting

From light fabric cut:
- 1 (5¼") A square then cut twice diagonally ◻
- 2 (2⅞") B squares then cut once diagonally ◻
- 1 (3⅜") C square

From dark fabric cut:
- 8 (2⅞") D squares then cut once diagonally ◻

Completing the Block

1. Stitch one B HST and one D HST together as shown in Figure 1. Press. Make 4.

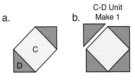

Figure 1   **Figure 2**

2. Stitch one D HST to each side of an A QST as shown in Figure 2. Press. Make 4.

3. Stitch one D HST to opposite sides of the C square as shown in Figure 3a. Press. Stitch a D HST to the remaining two sides of C as shown in Figure 3b. Press.

a.   b.   C-D Unit
                  Make 1

Figure 3

4. Referring to the photo and Assembly Diagram, lay out all units as shown and stitch together to complete one block. Press.

Week No. 9: Connecticut
Assembly Diagram 8½" x 8½"

5. Layer backing right side down, battings and pot holder block right side up. Quilt as desired. Bind pot holder and make hanging loop referring to General Instructions on page 3. ●

Fortress

Finished Size
Pot Holder Size:
8½" x 8½"

Materials
- 1 (2½" x WOF) coordinating fabric for binding and loop
- Scrap light fabric
- Scrap dark fabric
- 10" x 10" backing
- 10" x 10" heat-resistant batting
- 10" x 10" cotton batting
- Thread
- Basic sewing tools and supplies

Project Notes
Read all instructions before beginning this project.

Stitch right sides together using a ¼" seam allowance unless otherwise specified.

Materials and cutting lists assume 40" of usable fabric width for yardage.

WOF – width of fabric
HST – half square triangle ◺
QST – quarter square triangle ⊠

Cutting

From light fabric cut:
- 1 (5¼") A square then cut twice diagonally ⊠
- 2 (2⅞") B squares then cut once diagonally ◺
- 1 (3⅜") C square

From dark fabric cut:
- 1 (5¼") D square then cut twice diagonally ⊠
- 4 (2⅞") E squares then cut once diagonally ◺

Completing the Block
1. Stitch one B HST and one E HST together as shown in Figure 1a. Press. Make 2. Reversing positions, stitch one E HST and one B HST together as shown in Figure 1b. Press. Make 2.

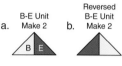

Figure 1

2. Stitch one D QST to each unit and reverse unit from step 1 as shown in Figure 2. Press. Make 2 each.

3. Stitch one E HST to each unit from step 2 as shown in Figure 3. Press. Make 2 each.

Figure 2   Figure 3

4. Referring to the photo and Assembly Diagram, lay out all units with C square as shown and stitch together to complete one block. Press.

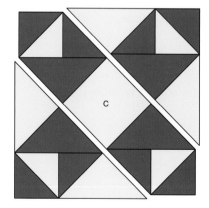

Week No. 10: Fortress
Assembly Diagram 8½" x 8½"

5. Layer backing right side down, battings and pot holder block right side up. Quilt as desired. Bind pot holder and make hanging loop referring to General Instructions on page 3. ●

Square in a Square

Finished Size

Pot Holder Size:
8½" x 8½"

Materials

- 1 (2½" x WOF) coordinating fabric for binding and loop
- Scrap light fabric
- Scrap dark fabric
- 10" x 10" backing
- 10" x 10" heat-resistant batting
- 10" x 10" cotton batting
- Thread
- Basic sewing tools and supplies

Project Notes

Read all instructions before beginning this project.

Stitch right sides together using a ¼" seam allowance unless otherwise specified.

Materials and cutting lists assume 40" of usable fabric width for yardage.

WOF – width of fabric
HST – half square triangle ◻
QST – quarter square triangle ⊠

Cutting

From light fabric cut:

- 1 (6½") A square

From dark fabric cut:

- 2 (4⅞") B squares then cut once diagonally ◻

Completing the Block

1. Referring to the photo and Assembly Diagram, lay out all pieces as shown and stitch together to complete one block. Press.

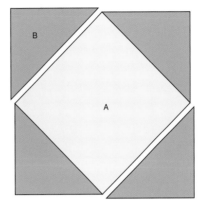

Week No. 11: Square in a Square
Assembly Diagram 8½" x 8½"

2. Layer backing right side down, battings and pot holder block right side up. Quilt as desired. Bind pot holder and make hanging loop referring to General Instructions on page 3.

Optional Center Square Finish

This is a great block to add a personalized option to. You can add an appliqué to the middle square or stitch in a meaningful word, saying or message. In the example given for this block, a simple flower was appliquéd to the center. You'll find several possible appliqué patterns to use throughout this book, or feel free to make your own. Refer to the General Instructions on page 3 for appliqué techniques. ●

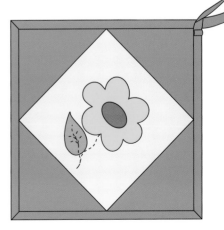

Week No. 11 Option: Flower Appliqué
Placement Diagram 8½" x 8½"

Week No. 11 Option: Square in a Square
Flower Appliqué Motif

Dutchman's Puzzle

Finished Size
Pot Holder Size:
8½" x 8½"

Materials
- 1 (2½" x WOF) coordinating fabric for binding and loop
- Scrap light fabric
- Scrap dark fabric
- 10" x 10" backing
- 10" x 10" heat-resistant batting
- 10" x 10" cotton batting
- Thread
- Basic sewing tools and supplies

Project Notes
Read all instructions before beginning this project.

Stitch right sides together using a ¼" seam allowance unless otherwise specified.

Materials and cutting lists assume 40" of usable fabric width for yardage.

WOF – width of fabric
HST – half square triangle □
QST – quarter square triangle ⊠

Cutting

From light fabric cut:
- 8 (2⅞") A squares then cut once diagonally □

From dark fabric cut:
- 2 (5¼") B squares then cut twice diagonally ⊠

Completing the Block

1. Stitch one A HST to each side of a B QST as shown in Figure 1. Press. Make 8.

A-B Unit
Make 8

Figure 1

2. Stitch two units from step 1 together as shown in Figure 2. Press. Make 4.

Quarter Block Unit
Make 4

Figure 2

3. Referring to the photo and Assembly Diagram, lay out all units as shown and stitch together to complete one block. Press.

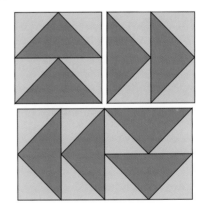

Week No. 12: Dutchman's Puzzle
Assembly Diagram 8½" x 8½"

4. Layer backing right side down, battings and pot holder block right side up. Quilt as desired. Bind pot holder and make hanging loop referring to General Instructions on page 3. ●

Square Me Up

Finished Size

Pot Holder Size:
8½" x 8½"

Materials

- 1 (2½" x WOF) coordinating fabric for binding and loop
- Scrap light fabric
- Scrap dark fabric
- 10" x 10" backing
- 10" x 10" heat-resistant batting
- 10" x 10" cotton batting
- Thread
- Basic sewing tools and supplies

Project Notes

Read all instructions before beginning this project.

Stitch right sides together using a ¼" seam allowance unless otherwise specified.

Materials and cutting lists assume 40" of usable fabric width for yardage.

WOF – width of fabric
HST – half square triangle
QST – quarter square triangle

Cutting

From light fabric cut:

- 2 (4⅞") A squares then cut once diagonally
- 1 (4½") B square

From dark fabric cut:

- 1 (5¼") C square then cut twice diagonally

Completing the Block

1. Stitch one C QST to opposite sides of the B square as shown in Figure 1. Press.

B-C Unit

Figure 1

2. Stitch one C QST to the remaining two sides of the unit from step 1 as shown in Figure 2. Press.

3. Referring to the photo and Assembly Diagram, stitch one A HST to each opposite side of the unit from step 2, and one A HST to the remaining sides to complete one block. Press.

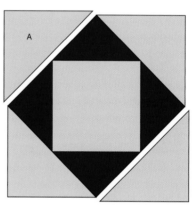

Figure 2

Week No. 13: Square Me Up
Assembly Diagram 8½" x 8½"

4. Layer backing right side down, battings and pot holder block right side up. Quilt as desired. Bind pot holder and make hanging loop referring to General Instructions on page 3.

Example of Poor Color Selection

Here's an example of how a block design can be lost if there isn't enough contrast between the fabrics used. The two pinks used for this pot holder were too similar in color so the piecing was lost. Pick your fabrics wisely and look for good contrast. Lights and darks work best.

Leaf Appliqué Option

This is a great block to add a personalized option to. You can add an appliqué to the middle unit or stitch in a meaningful word, saying or message. In the example given for this block, a three-leaved motif has been appliquéd to the center. You'll find several possible appliqué patterns to use throughout this book, or feel free to make your own. Refer to the General Instructions on page 3 for appliqué techniques. ●

Week No. 13 Option: Leaf Appliqué
Placement Diagram 8¹/₂" x 8¹/₂"

Week No. 13 Option: Square Me Up
Leaf Appliqué

Week No.14

Double X

Finished Size

Pot Holder Size:
8½" x 8½"

Materials

- 1 (2½" x WOF) coordinating fabric for binding and loop
- Scrap light fabric
- Scrap dark fabric
- 10" x 10" backing
- 10" x 10" heat-resistant batting
- 10" x 10" cotton batting
- Thread
- Basic sewing tools and supplies

Project Notes

Read all instructions before beginning this project.

Stitch right sides together using a ¼" seam allowance unless otherwise specified.

Materials and cutting lists assume 40" of usable fabric width for yardage.

WOF – width of fabric
HST – half square triangle ◻
QST – quarter square triangle ⊠

Cutting

From light fabric cut:

- 1 (4½") A square
- 5 (2⅞") B squares then cut once diagonally ◻
- 2 (2½") C squares

From dark fabric cut:

- 5 (2⅞") D squares then cut once diagonally ◻

Completing the Block

1. Stitch one B HST and one D HST together as shown in Figure 1. Press. Make 10.

B-D Unit
Make 10

Figure 1

2. Stitch two units from step 1 together as shown in Figure 2. Press. Make 2.

Side Unit
Make 2

Figure 2

3. Stitch three units from step 1 and one C square together as shown in Figure 3. Press. Make 2.

Top/Bottom Unit
Make 2

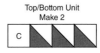

Figure 3

4. Referring to the photo and Assembly Diagram, lay out all units and the A square as shown and stitch together to complete one block. Press.

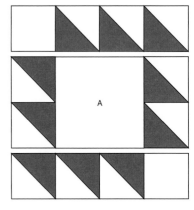

Week No. 14: Double X
Assembly Diagram 8½" x 8½"

5. Layer backing right side down, battings and pot holder block right side up. Quilt as desired. Bind pot holder and make hanging loop referring to General Instructions on page 3.

Optional Center Square Finish

This is a great block to add a personalized option to. You can add an appliqué to the middle block or stitch in a meaningful word, saying or message. In the example given for this block, a little chickadee was appliquéd to the center. You'll find several possible appliqué patterns to use throughout this book, or feel free to make your own. Refer to the General Instructions on page 3 for appliqué techniques. ●

Week No. 14 Option: Chickadee Appliqué
Placement Diagram 8¹⁄₂" x 8¹⁄₂"

Week No. 14 Option: Double X
Chickadee Appliqué

Electric Fan

Finished Size

Pot Holder Size:
8½" x 8½"

Materials

- 1 (2½" x WOF) coordinating fabric for binding and loop
- Scrap light fabric
- Scrap medium fabric
- Scrap dark fabric
- 10" x 10" backing
- 10" x 10" heat-resistant batting
- 10" x 10" cotton batting
- Thread
- Basic sewing tools and supplies

Project Notes

Read all instructions before beginning this project.

Stitch right sides together using a ¼" seam allowance unless otherwise specified.

Materials and cutting lists assume 40" of usable fabric width for yardage.

WOF – width of fabric
HST – half square triangle ◻
QST – quarter square triangle ⊠

Cutting

From light fabric cut:

- 2 (5¼") A squares then cut twice diagonally ⊠

From medium fabric cut:

- 1 (5¼") B square then cut twice diagonally ⊠

From dark fabric cut:

- 1 (5¼") C square then cut twice diagonally ⊠

Completing the Block

1. Stitch one A QST and one C QST together as shown in Figure 1. Press. Make 4.

A-C Unit
Make 4

Figure 1

2. Stitch one A QST and one B QST together as shown in Figure 2. Press. Make 4.

A-B Unit
Make 4

Figure 2

3. Stitch one unit from step 1 and one unit from step 2 together as shown in Figure 3. Press. Make 4.

Quarter Block Unit
Make 4

Figure 3

4. Referring to the photo and Assembly Diagram, lay out all units as shown and stitch together to complete one block. Press.

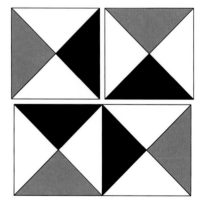

Week No. 15: Electric Fan
Assembly Diagram 8½" x 8½"

5. Layer backing right side down, battings and pot holder block right side up. Quilt as desired. Bind pot holder and make hanging loop referring to General Instructions on page 3. ●

Bow Ties & Checks

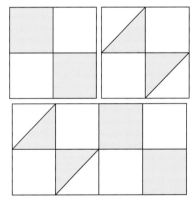

Finished Size

Pot Holder Size:
8½" x 8½"

Materials

- 1 (2½" x WOF) coordinating fabric for binding and loop
- Scrap light fabric
- Scrap dark fabric
- 10" x 10" backing
- 10" x 10" heat-resistant batting
- 10" x 10" cotton batting
- Thread
- Basic sewing tools and supplies

Project Notes

Read all instructions before beginning this project.

Stitch right sides together using a ¼" seam allowance unless otherwise specified.

Materials and cutting lists assume 40" of usable fabric width for yardage.

WOF – width of fabric
HST – half square triangle ◻
QST – quarter square triangle ◻

Cutting

From light fabric cut:

- 2 (2⅞") A squares then cut once diagonally ◻
- 8 (2½") B squares

From dark fabric cut:

- 2 (2⅞") C squares then cut once diagonally ◻
- 4 (2½") D squares

Completing the Block

1. Stitch one A HST and one C HST together as shown in Figure 1. Press. Make 4.

A-C Unit
Make 4

C / A

Figure 1

2. Stitch one unit from step 1 and one B square together as shown in Figure 2. Press. Make 4.

A-B-E Unit
Make 4

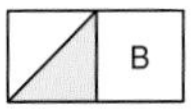

Make 2

Figure 2   **Figure 3**

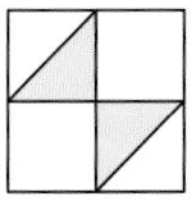

3. Stitch two units from step 2 together as shown in Figure 3. Press. Make 2.

4. Stitch one B and one D square together as shown in Figure 4. Press. Make 4.

B-D Unit
Make 4

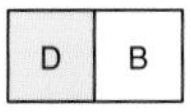

D   B

Figure 4

5. Stitch two units from step 4 together as shown in Figure 5. Press. Make 2.

Four-Patch Unit
Make 2

Figure 5

6. Referring to the photo and Assembly Diagram, lay out all units as shown and stitch together to complete one block. Press.

Week No. 16: Bow Ties & Checks
Assembly Diagram 8½" x 8½"

7. Layer backing right side down, battings and pot holder block right side up. Quilt as desired. Bind pot holder and make hanging loop referring to General Instructions on page 3. ●

Week No. 17

Crystal Star

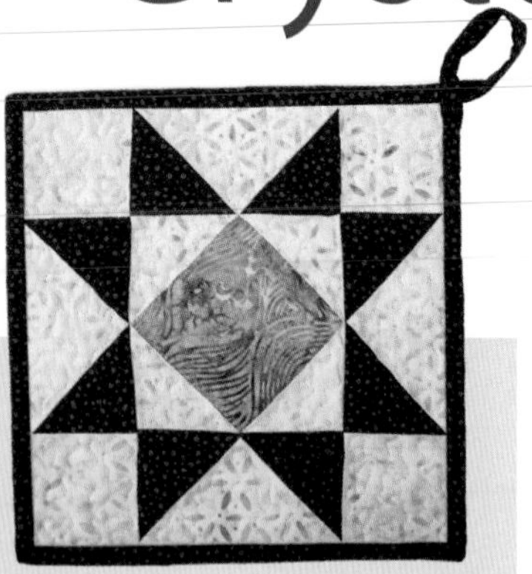

Finished Size

Pot Holder Size:
8½" x 8½"

Materials

- 1 (2½" x WOF) coordinating fabric for binding and loop
- Scrap light fabric
- Scrap medium fabric
- Scrap dark fabric
- 10" x 10" backing
- 10" x 10" heat-resistant batting
- 10" x 10" cotton batting
- Thread
- Basic sewing tools and supplies

Project Notes

Read all instructions before beginning this project.

Stitch right sides together using a ¼" seam allowance unless otherwise specified.

Materials and cutting lists assume 40" of usable fabric width for yardage.

WOF – width of fabric
HST – half square triangle
QST – quarter square triangle

Cutting

From light fabric cut:

- 1 (5¼") A square then cut twice diagonally
- 2 (2⅞") B squares then cut once diagonally
- 4 (2½") C squares

From medium fabric cut:

- 1 (3⅜") D square

From dark fabric cut:

- 4 (2⅞") E squares then cut once diagonally

Completing the Block

1. Stitch one B HST to opposite sides of a D square as shown in Figure 1a. Press. Stitch one B HST to each of the remaining sides as shown in Figure 1b. Press.

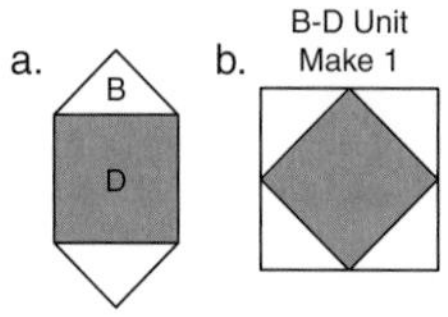
a.
B
D
b.
B-D Unit
Make 1

Figure 1

2. Stitch one E HST to each side of an A QST as shown in Figure 2. Press. Make 4.

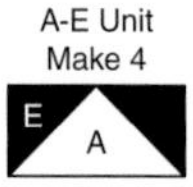
A-E Unit
Make 4
E
A

Figure 2

3. Referring to the photo and Assembly Diagram, lay out all units and C squares as shown and stitch together to complete one block. Press.

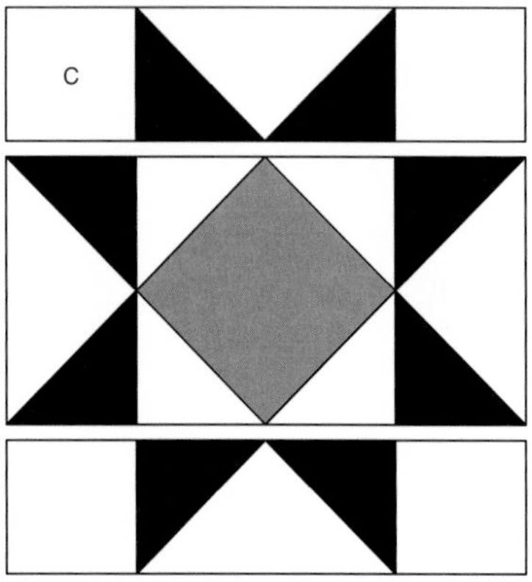
C

Week No. 17: Crystal Star
Assembly Diagram 8½" x 8½"

4. Layer backing right side down, battings and pot holder block right side up. Quilt as desired. Bind pot holder and make hanging loop referring to General Instructions on page 3.

Crosses & Losses

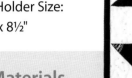

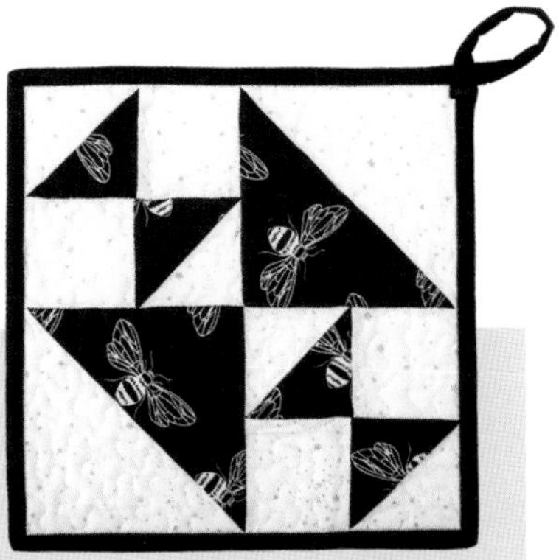

Finished Size

Pot Holder Size:
8½" x 8½"

Materials

- 1 (2½" x WOF) coordinating fabric for binding and loop
- Scrap light fabric
- Scrap dark fabric
- 10" x 10" backing
- 10" x 10" heat-resistant batting
- 10" x 10" cotton batting
- Thread
- Basic sewing tools and supplies

Project Notes

Read all instructions before beginning this project.

Stitch right sides together using a ¼" seam allowance unless otherwise specified.

Materials and cutting lists assume 40" of usable fabric width for yardage.

WOF – width of fabric
HST – half square triangle
QST – quarter square triangle

Cutting

From light fabric cut:

- 1 (4⅞") A square then cut once diagonally ◻
- 2 (2⅞") B squares then cut once diagonally ◻
- 4 (2½") C squares

From dark fabric cut:

- 1 (4⅞") D square then cut once diagonally ◻
- 2 (2⅞") E squares then cut once diagonally ◻

Completing the Block

1. Stitch one B HST and one E HST together as shown in Figure 1. Press open. Make 4.

B-E Unit
Make 4

Figure 1

B-C-E Unit
Make 4

Figure 2

2. Stitch one unit from step 1 to one C square as shown in Figure 2. Press. Make 4.

3. Stitch two units from step 2 together as shown in Figure 3. Press. Make 2.

Bow-Tie Unit
Make 2

Figure 3

A-D Unit
Make 2

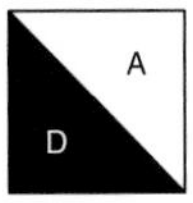

Figure 4

4. Stitch one A HST and one D HST together as shown in Figure 4. Press. Make 2.

5. Referring to the photo and Assembly Diagram, lay out all units as shown and stitch together to complete one block. Press.

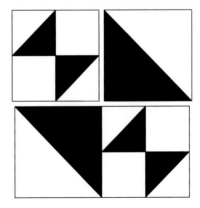

Week No. 18: Crosses & Losses
Assembly Diagram 8½" x 8½"

6. Layer backing right side down, battings and pot holder block right side up. Quilt as desired. Bind pot holder and make hanging loop referring to General Instructions on page 3. ●

Cross in a Square

Finished Size

Pot Holder Size:
8½" x 8½"

Materials

- 1 (2½" x WOF) coordinating fabric for binding and loop
- Scrap light fabric
- Scrap medium fabric
- Scrap dark fabric
- 10" x 10" backing
- 10" x 10" heat-resistant batting
- 10" x 10" cotton batting
- Thread
- Basic sewing tools and supplies

Project Notes

Read all instructions before beginning this project.

Stitch right sides together using a ¼" seam allowance unless otherwise specified.

Materials and cutting lists assume 40" of usable fabric width for yardage.

WOF – width of fabric
HST – half square triangle ◱
QST – quarter square triangle ⊠

Cutting

From light fabric cut:

- 5 (2½") A squares

From medium fabric cut:

- 6 (2½") B squares

From dark fabric cut:

- 5 (2½") C squares

Completing the Block

1. Stitch three A and one B square as shown in Figure 1. Press.

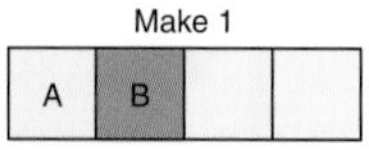

Make 1

Figure 1

2. Stitch two B and one each A and C squares together as shown in Figure 2. Press. Make 2.

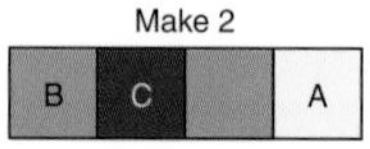

Make 2

Figure 2

3. Stitch one B square and three C squares together as shown in Figure 3. Press.

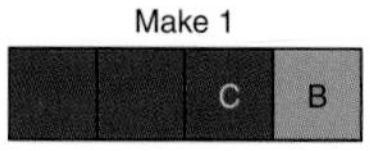

Make 1

Figure 3

4. Referring to the photo and Assembly Diagram, lay out all units as shown and stitch together to complete one block. Press.

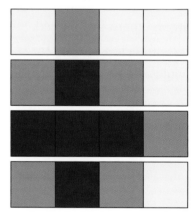

Week No. 19: Cross in a Square
Assembly Diagram 8½" x 8½"

5. Layer backing right side down, battings and pot holder block right side up. Quilt as desired. Bind pot holder and make hanging loop referring to General Instructions on page 3. ●

Diana's Dart

Finished Size
Pot Holder Size:
8½" x 8½"

Materials
- 1 (2½" x WOF) coordinating fabric for binding and loop
- Scrap light fabric
- Scrap dark fabric
- 10" x 10" backing
- 10" x 10" heat-resistant batting
- 10" x 10" cotton batting
- Thread
- Basic sewing tools and supplies

Project Notes
Read all instructions before beginning this project.

Stitch right sides together using a ¼" seam allowance unless otherwise specified.

Materials and cutting lists assume 40" of usable fabric width for yardage.

WOF – width of fabric
HST – half square triangle ◻
QST – quarter square triangle ⊠

Cutting

From light fabric cut:
- 5 (2⅞") A squares then cut once diagonally ◻

From dark fabric cut:
- 1 (4⅞") B square then cut once diagonally ◻
- 3 (2⅞") C squares then cut once diagonally ◻
- 4 (2½") D squares

Completing the Block

1. Stitch one A HST and one C HST together as shown in Figure 1. Press open. Make 6.

A-C Unit Make 6

Figure 1

2. Stitch one unit from step 1 and one D square as shown in Figure 2. Press. Make 4.

A-C-D Unit Make 4

Figure 2

Bow-Tie Unit Make 2

Figure 3

3. Stitch two units from step 2 together as shown in Figure 3. Press. Make 2.

4. Stitch one A HST to two sides of a unit from step 1 as shown in Figure 4. Press. Make 2.

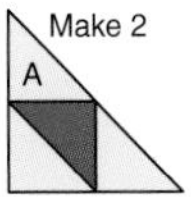

Make 2

Figure 4

Make 2

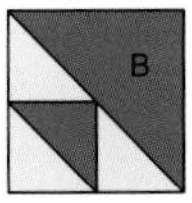

Figure 5

5. Stitch a B HST to a unit from step 4 as shown in Figure 5. Press. Make 2.

6. Referring to the photo and Assembly Diagram, lay out all units as shown and stitch together to complete one block. Press.

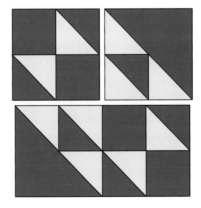

Week No. 20: Diana's Dart
Assembly Diagram 8½" x 8½"

7. Layer backing right side down, battings and pot holder block right side up. Quilt as desired. Bind pot holder and make hanging loop referring to General Instructions on page 3. ●

Rotating Star

Finished Size

Pot Holder Size:
8½" x 8½"

Materials

- 1 (2½" x WOF) coordinating fabric for binding and loop
- Scrap light fabric
- Scrap medium fabric
- Scrap dark fabric
- 10" x 10" backing
- 10" x 10" heat-resistant batting
- 10" x 10" cotton batting
- Thread
- Basic sewing tools and supplies

Project Notes

Read all instructions before beginning this project.

Stitch right sides together using a ¼" seam allowance unless otherwise specified.

Materials and cutting lists assume 40" of usable fabric width for yardage.

WOF – width of fabric
HST – half square triangle
QST – quarter square triangle

Cutting

From light fabric cut:

- 1 (5¼") A square then cut twice diagonally
- 1 (3¼") B square then cut twice diagonally
- 4 (2½") C squares

From medium fabric cut:

- 2 (2⅞") D squares then cut once diagonally

From dark fabric cut:

- 1 (3¼") E square then cut twice diagonally
- 4 (2⅞") F squares then cut once diagonally

Completing the Block

1. Stitch one B QST and one E QST together as shown in Figure 1. Press. Make 4.

B-E Unit
Make 4

B-D-E Unit
Make 4

Figure 1   **Figure 2**

2. Stitch one unit from step 1 and one D HST as shown in Figure 2. Press. Make 4.

3. Stitch the four units from step 2 together as shown in Figure 3. Press.

Center Unit
Make 1

A-F Unit
Make 4

Figure 3   **Figure 4**

4. Stitch one F HST to each side of an A QST as shown in Figure 4. Press. Make 4.

5. Referring to the photo and Assembly Diagram, lay out all units and C squares as shown and stitch together to complete one block. Press.

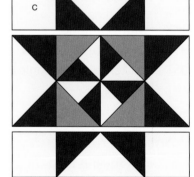

Week No. 21: Rotating Star
Assembly Diagram 8½" x 8½"

6. Layer backing right side down, battings and pot holder block right side up. Quilt as desired. Bind pot holder and make hanging loop referring to General Instructions on page 3. ●

Economy Block

Finished Size
Pot Holder Size:
8½" x 8½"

Materials
- 1 (2½" x WOF) coordinating fabric for binding and loop
- Scrap light No. 1 fabric
- Scrap light No. 2 fabric
- Scrap medium No. 1 fabric
- Scrap medium No. 2 fabric
- Scrap dark fabric
- 10" x 10" backing
- 10" x 10" heat-resistant batting
- 10" x 10" cotton batting
- Thread
- Basic sewing tools and supplies

Project Notes
Read all instructions before beginning this project.

Stitch right sides together using a ¼" seam allowance unless otherwise specified.

Materials and cutting lists assume 40" of usable fabric width for yardage.

WOF – width of fabric
HST – half square triangle ◻
QST – quarter square triangle ⊠

Cutting

From light No. 1 fabric cut:
- 2 (2⅞") A squares then cut once diagonally ◻

From light No. 2 fabric cut:
- 1 (5¼") B square then cut twice diagonally ⊠

From medium No. 1 fabric cut:
- 1 (5¼") C square then cut twice diagonally ⊠

From medium No. 2 fabric cut:
- 1 (3⅜") D square

From dark fabric cut:
- 1 (5¼") E square then cut twice diagonally ⊠

Completing the Block

1. Stitch one A HST to opposite sides of the D square as shown in Figure 1. Press. Stitch one A HST to the remaining two sides of D.

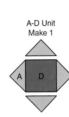

A-D Unit
Make 1

Center Unit
Make 1

Figure 1

Figure 2

2. Stitch one E QST to opposite sides of the unit from step 1 as shown in Figure 2. Press. Stitch one E QST to the remaining two sides. Press.

3. Stitch one B QST and one C QST together as shown in Figure 3. Press. Make 4.

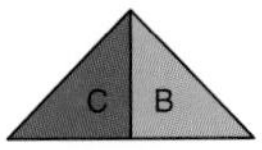

B-C Unit
Make 4

Figure 3

4. Referring to the photo and Assembly Diagram, lay out all units as shown and stitch together to complete one block. Press.

Week No. 22: Economy Block
Assembly Diagram 8½" x 8½"

5. Layer backing right side down, battings and pot holder block right side up. Quilt as desired. Bind pot holder and make hanging loop referring to General Instructions on page 3. ●

Week No. 23

Double Four-Patch

Finished Size

Pot Holder Size:
8½" x 8½"

Materials

- 1 (2½" x WOF) coordinating fabric for binding and loop
- Scrap light fabric
- Scrap dark fabric
- 10" x 10" backing
- 10" x 10" heat-resistant batting
- 10" x 10" cotton batting
- Thread
- Basic sewing tools and supplies

Project Notes

Read all instructions before beginning this project.

Stitch right sides together using a ¼" seam allowance unless otherwise specified.

Materials and cutting lists assume 40" of usable fabric width for yardage.

WOF – width of fabric
HST – half square triangle ◻
QST – quarter square triangle ⊠

Cutting

From light fabric cut:

- 2 (4½") A squares
- 4 (2½") B squares

From dark fabric cut:

- 4 (2½") C squares

Completing the Block

1. Stitch one B and one C square together as shown in Figure 1. Press. Make 4.

B-C Unit
Make 4

| B | C |

Figure 1

2. Stitch two units from step 1 together as shown in Figure 2. Press. Make 2.

Four-Patch Unit
Make 2

Figure 2

3. Referring to the photo and Assembly Diagram, lay out all units and A squares as shown and stitch together to complete one block. Press.

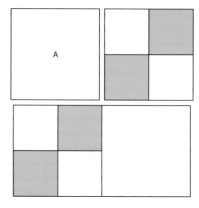

Week No. 23: Double Four-Patch
Assembly Diagram 8½" x 8½"

4. Layer backing right side down, battings and pot holder block right side up. Quilt as desired. Bind pot holder and make hanging loop referring to General Instructions on page 3. ●

This Way Home

Finished Size

Pot Holder Size:
8½" x 8½"

Materials

- 1 (2½" x WOF) coordinating fabric for binding and loop
- Scrap light fabric
- Scrap dark fabric
- 10" x 10" backing
- 10" x 10" heat-resistant batting
- 10" x 10" cotton batting
- Thread
- Basic sewing tools and supplies

Project Notes

Read all instructions before beginning this project.

Stitch right sides together using a ¼" seam allowance unless otherwise specified.

Materials and cutting lists assume 40" of usable fabric width for yardage.

WOF – width of fabric
HST – half square triangle
QST – quarter square triangle

Cutting

From light fabric cut:

- 1 (4½") A square
- 4 (2⅞") B squares then cut once diagonally
- 2 (2½") C squares

From dark fabric cut:

- 4 (2⅞") D squares then cut once diagonally
- 2 (2½") E squares

Completing the Block

1. Stitch one B HST and one D HST together as shown in Figure 1. Press. Make 8.

B-D Unit
Make 8

B
D

Figure 1

2. Stitch two units from step 1 together as shown in Figure 2a. Press. Make 2. Make reversed units, again referring to Figure 2b. Press. Make 2.

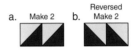

a. Make 2   b. Reversed Make 2

Figure 2

3. Stitch one C and one E square to each end of the first units from step 2 as shown in Figure 3. Press. Make 2.

Make 2

C   E

Figure 3

4. Referring to the photo and Assembly Diagram, lay out all units and the A square as shown and stitch together to complete one block. Press.

A

Week No. 24: This Way Home
Assembly Diagram 8½" x 8½"

5. Layer backing right side down, battings and pot holder block right side up. Quilt as desired. Bind pot holder and make hanging loop referring to General Instructions on page 3.

Optional Center Block Finish

This is a great block to add a personalized option to. You can add an appliqué to the middle block or stitch in a meaningful word, saying or message.

In the example given for this block, a coffee cup was appliquéd to the center. Then, for an added touch, "Boss" was free-motion quilted on the cup. You'll find several possible appliqué patterns to use throughout this book, or feel free to make your own. Refer to the General Instructions on page 3 for appliqué and quilted words techniques. ●

Week No. 24 Option: Coffee Cup Appliqué
Placement Diagram 8½" x 8½"

Week No. 24 Option: This Way Home
Coffee Cup Appliqué

My Flower Basket

Finished Size

Pot Holder Size:
8½" x 8½"

Materials

- 1 (2½" x WOF) coordinating fabric for binding and loop
- Scrap light fabric
- Scrap dark fabric
- 10" x 10" backing
- 10" x 10" heat-resistant batting
- 10" x 10" cotton batting
- Thread
- Basic sewing tools and supplies

Project Notes

Read all instructions before beginning this project.

Stitch right sides together using a ¼" seam allowance unless otherwise specified.

Materials and cutting lists assume 40" of usable fabric width for yardage.

WOF – width of fabric
HST – half square triangle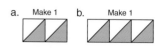
QST – quarter square triangle

Cutting

From light fabric cut:

- 1 (4⅞") A square then cut once diagonally
- 2 (2½" x 4½") B rectangles
- 4 (2⅞") C squares then cut once diagonally

From dark fabric cut:

- 1 (4⅞") D square then cut once diagonally
- 4 (2⅞") E squares then cut once diagonally

Completing the Block

1. Stitch one C HST and one E HST together as shown in Figure 1. Press. Make 6.

C-E Unit
Make 6

a. Make 1   b. Make 1

Figure 1

Figure 2

2. Stitch two units from step 1 together as shown in Figure 2a. Press. Stitch three units from step 1 together as shown in Figure 2b. Press.

3. Stitch one E HST to one B rectangle as shown in Figure 3a. Press. Stitch one E HST to one B rectangle as shown in Figure 3b. Press.

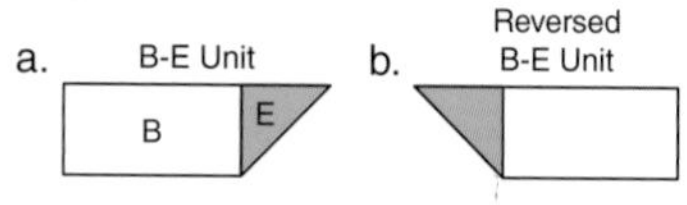

a. B-E Unit   b. Reversed B-E Unit

Figure 3

4. Stitch one C HST to two sides of a unit from step 1 as shown in Figure 4. Press.

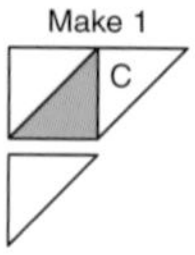

Make 1

Figure 4

5. Referring to the photo and Assembly Diagram, lay out all units and D and A pieces as shown and stitch together to complete one block. Press.

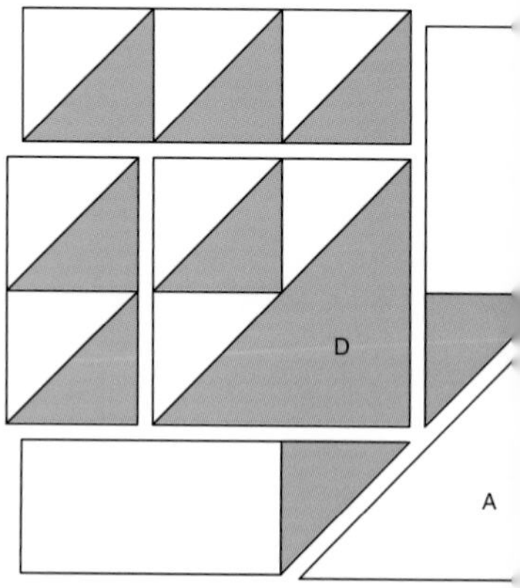

6. Layer backing right side down, battings and pot holder block right side up. Quilt as desired. Bind pot holder and make hanging loop referring to General Instructions on page 3.

Week No. 25: My Flower Basket
Assembly Diagram 8½" x 8½"

Optional Center Square Finish

This is a great block to add a personalized option to. You can add an appliqué to the middle block or stitch in a meaningful word, saying or message. In the example given for this block, a couple of flowers and leaves were appliquéd to the center over the basket block. Refer to the General Instructions on page 3 for appliqué techniques. ●

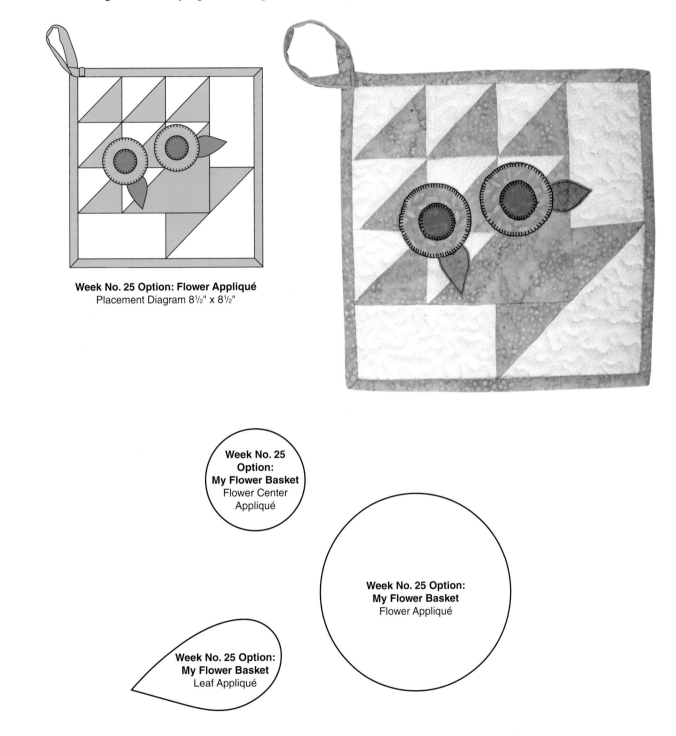

Week No. 25 Option: Flower Appliqué
Placement Diagram 8½" x 8½"

**Week No. 25
Option:
My Flower Basket**
Flower Center
Appliqué

**Week No. 25 Option:
My Flower Basket**
Flower Appliqué

**Week No. 25 Option:
My Flower Basket**
Leaf Appliqué

Triangle Affair

Finished Size
Pot Holder Size:
8½" x 8½"

Materials
- 1 (2½" x WOF) coordinating fabric for binding and loop
- Scrap light fabric
- Scrap dark fabric
- 10" x 10" backing
- 10" x 10" heat-resistant batting
- 10" x 10" cotton batting
- Thread
- Basic sewing tools and supplies

Project Notes
Read all instructions before beginning this project.

Stitch right sides together using a ¼" seam allowance unless otherwise specified.

Materials and cutting lists assume 40" of usable fabric width for yardage.

WOF – width of fabric
HST – half square triangle
QST – quarter square triangle ⊠

Cutting

From light fabric cut:
- 1 (4⅞") A square then cut once diagonally ◻
- 4 (2⅞") B squares then cut once diagonally ◻

From dark fabric cut:
- 1 (4⅞") C square then cut once diagonally ◻
- 4 (2⅞") D squares then cut once diagonally ◻

Completing the Block
1. Stitch one B HST and one D HST together as shown in Figure 1. Press. Make 8.

B-D Unit
Make 8

Make 4

Figure 1   **Figure 2**

2. Stitch two units from step 1 together as shown in Figure 2. Press. Make 4.

3. Stitch two units from step 2 together as shown in Figure 3. Press. Make 2.

Make 2

A-C Unit
Make 2

Figure 3   **Figure 4**

4. Stitch one A HST and one C HST together as shown in Figure 4. Press. Make 2.

5. Referring to the photo and Assembly Diagram, lay out all units as shown and stitch together to complete one block. Press.

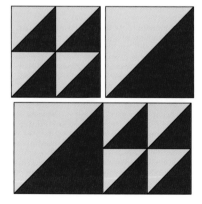

Week No. 26: Triangle Affair
Assembly Diagram 8½" x 8½"

6. Layer backing right side down, battings and pot holder block right side up. Quilt as desired. Bind pot holder and make hanging loop referring to General Instructions on page 3. ●

Moon Glow

Finished Size
Pot Holder Size:
8½" x 8½"

Materials
- 1 (2½" x WOF) coordinating fabric for binding and loop
- Scrap light fabric
- Scrap light-medium fabric
- Scrap medium fabric
- Scrap dark fabric
- 10" x 10" backing
- 10" x 10" heat-resistant batting
- 10" x 10" cotton batting
- Thread
- Basic sewing tools and supplies

Project Notes
Read all instructions before beginning this project.

Stitch right sides together using a ¼" seam allowance unless otherwise specified.

Materials and cutting lists assume 40" of usable fabric width for yardage.

WOF – width of fabric
HST – half square triangle
QST – quarter square triangle

Cutting

From light fabric cut:
- 5 (2⅞") A squares then cut once diagonally

From light-medium fabric cut:
- 2 (2⅞") B squares then cut once diagonally
- 2 (2½") C squares

From medium fabric cut:
- 1 (4⅞") D square then cut once diagonally

From dark fabric cut:
- 1 (2⅞") E square then cut once diagonally
- 2 (2½") F squares

Completing the Block

1. Stitch one A HST and one B HST together as shown in Figure 1. Press. Make 4.

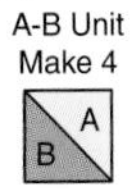

A-B Unit
Make 4

A-E Unit
Make 2

Figure 1    **Figure 2**

2. Stitch one A HST and one E HST together as shown in Figure 2. Press. Make 2.

3. Stitch one C square and one F square to two units from step 1 as shown in Figure 3. Press. Make 2.

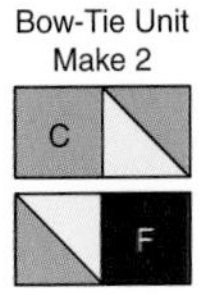

Bow-Tie Unit
Make 2

Make 2

Figure 3 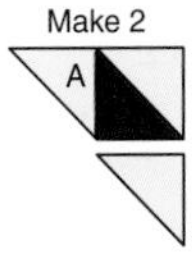   **Figure 4**

4. Stitch one A HST to side and bottom of a unit from step 2 as shown in Figure 4. Press. Make 2.

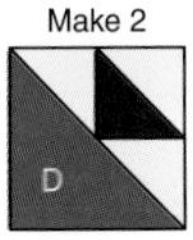

Make 2

5. Stitch a D HST to a unit from step 4 as shown in Figure 5. Press. Make 2.

Figure 5

6. Referring to the photo and Assembly Diagram, lay out all units as shown and stitch together to complete one block. Press.

Week No. 27: Moon Glow
Assembly Diagram 8½" x 8½"

7. Layer backing right side down, battings and pot holder block right side up. Quilt as desired. Bind pot holder and make hanging loop referring to General Instructions on page 3. ●

Fair & Square

Finished Size

Pot Holder Size:
8½" x 8½"

Materials

- 1 (2½" x WOF) coordinating fabric for binding and loop
- Scrap very light fabric
- Scrap light fabric
- Scrap medium fabric
- Scrap dark fabric
- 10" x 10" backing
- 10" x 10" heat-resistant batting
- 10" x 10" cotton batting
- Thread
- Basic sewing tools and supplies

Project Notes

Read all instructions before beginning this project.

Stitch right sides together using a ¼" seam allowance unless otherwise specified.

Materials and cutting lists assume 40" of usable fabric width for yardage.

WOF – width of fabric

HST – half square triangle

QST – quarter square triangle ⊠

Cutting

From very light fabric cut:

- 4 (2½" x 4½") A rectangles

From light fabric cut:

- 1 (2⅞") B square then cut once diagonally ◹
- 4 (2½") C squares

From medium fabric cut:

- 1 (2⅞") D square then cut once diagonally ◹

From dark fabric cut:

- 2 (2⅞") E squares then cut once diagonally ◹

Completing the Block

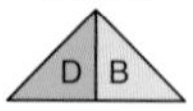

1. Stitch one B HST and one D HST together as shown in Figure 1. Press. Make 2.

B-D Unit
Make 2

Figure 1

2. Stitch the two units from step 1 together as shown in Figure 2. Press.

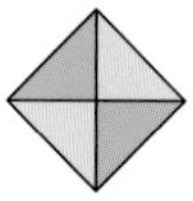

Hourglass Unit
Make 1

Center Unit
Make 1

Figure 2 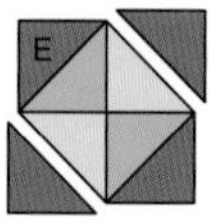   **Figure 3**

3. Stitch one E HST to opposite sides of the unit from step 2 as shown in Figure 3. Press. Stitch one E HST to the remaining two sides. Press.

4. Stitch C squares to each end of an A rectangle as shown in Figure 4. Press. Make 2.

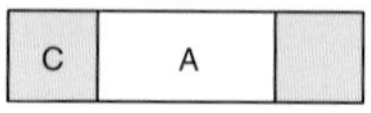

A-C Unit
Make 2

| C | A | |

Figure 4

5. Referring to the photo and Assembly Diagram, lay out all units as shown and stitch together to complete one block. Press.

6. Layer backing right side down, battings and pot holder block right side up. Quilt as desired. Bind pot holder and make hanging loop referring to General Instructions on page 3. ●

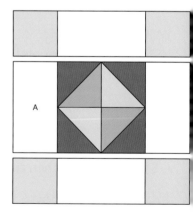

Week No. 28: Fair & Square
Assembly Diagram 8½" x 8½"

Ollie's Square

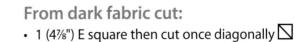

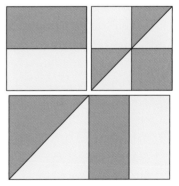

Finished Size

Pot Holder Size:
8½" x 8½"

Materials

- 1 (2½" x WOF) coordinating fabric for binding and loop
- Scrap light fabric
- Scrap dark fabric
- 10" x 10" backing
- 10" x 10" heat-resistant batting
- 10" x 10" cotton batting
- Thread
- Basic sewing tools and supplies

Project Notes

Read all instructions before beginning this project.

Stitch right sides together using a ¼" seam allowance unless otherwise specified.

Materials and cutting lists assume 40" of usable fabric width for yardage.

WOF – width of fabric
HST – half square triangle
QST – quarter square triangle

Cutting

Note: Cutting instructions will make two blocks.

From light fabric cut:

- 1 (4⅞") A square then cut once diagonally
- 4 (2½" x 4½") B rectangles
- 2 (2⅞") C squares then cut once diagonally
- 2 (2½") D squares

From dark fabric cut:

- 1 (4⅞") E square then cut once diagonally
- 4 (2½" x 4½") F rectangles
- 2 (2⅞") G squares then cut once diagonally
- 2 (2½") H squares

Completing the Block

1. Stitch one C HST and one G HST together as shown in Figure 1. Press. Make 2.

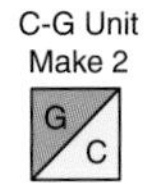

Figure 1

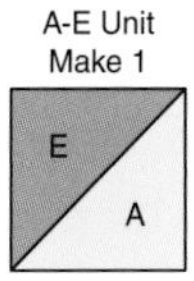

A-E Unit
Make 1

Figure 2

2. Stitch one A HST and one E HST together as shown in Figure 2. Press.

3. Stitch one B and one F rectangle together as shown in Figure 3. Press. Make 2.

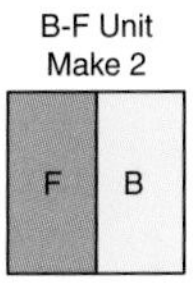

B-F Unit
Make 2

Figure 3

Quarter Unit
Make 1

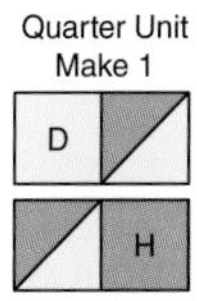

Figure 4

4. Stitch one D and one H square to two units from step 1 as shown in Figure 4. Press.

5. Referring to the photo and Assembly Diagram, lay out all units as shown and stitch together to complete one block. Press.

6. Repeat steps 1–5 to make a second block.

Week No. 29: Ollie's Square
Assembly Diagram 8½" x 8½"

7. For each block, layer backing right side down, battings and pot holder block right side up. Quilt as desired. Bind pot holders and make hanging loop referring to General Instructions on page 3. ●

Goose Tracks

Finished Size

Pot Holder Size:
8½" x 8½"

Materials

- 1 (2½" x WOF) coordinating fabric for binding and loop
- Scrap light fabric
- Scrap dark fabric
- 10" x 10" backing
- 10" x 10" heat-resistant batting
- 10" x 10" cotton batting
- Thread
- Basic sewing tools and supplies

Project Notes

Read all instructions before beginning this project.

Stitch right sides together using a ¼" seam allowance unless otherwise specified.

Materials and cutting lists assume 40" of usable fabric width for yardage.

WOF – width of fabric
HST – half square triangle
QST – quarter square triangle

Cutting

Note: Cutting instructions will make two blocks.

From light fabric cut:

- 1 (8⅞") A square then cut once diagonally
- 1 (4⅞") B square then cut once diagonally

From dark fabric cut:

- 3 (4⅞") C squares then cut once diagonally

Completing the Block

1. Stitch one B HST and one C HST together as shown in Figure 1. Press.

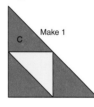

B-C Unit
Make 1

Figure 1

2. Stitch one C triangle to two sides of a unit from step 1 as shown in Figure 2. Press.

Make 1

Figure 2

3. Referring to the photo and Assembly Diagram, lay out the unit and A piece as shown and stitch together to complete one block. Press.

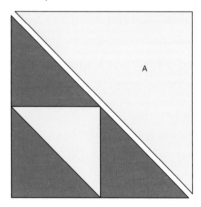

Week No. 30: Goose Tracks
Assembly Diagram 8½" x 8½"

4. Repeat steps 1–3 to make a second block.

5. For each block, layer backing right side down, battings and pot holder block right side up. Quilt as desired. Bind pot holders and make hanging loop referring to General Instructions on page 3. ●

Butterscotch Star

Finished Size
Pot Holder Size:
8½" x 8½"

Materials
- 1 (2½" x WOF) coordinating fabric for binding and loop
- Scrap light fabric
- Scrap dark fabric
- 10" x 10" backing
- 10" x 10" heat-resistant batting
- 10" x 10" cotton batting
- Thread
- Basic sewing tools and supplies

Project Notes
Read all instructions before beginning this project.

Stitch right sides together using a ¼" seam allowance unless otherwise specified.

Materials and cutting lists assume 40" of usable fabric width for yardage.

WOF – width of fabric
HST – half square triangle
QST – quarter square triangle

Cutting

From light fabric cut:
- 1 (5¼") A square then cut twice diagonally
- 1 (2⅞") B square then cut once diagonally
- 6 (2½") C squares

From dark fabric cut:
- 5 (2⅞") D squares then cut once diagonally

Completing the Block

1. Stitch one B HST and one D HST together as shown in Figure 1. Press. Make 2.

B-D Unit
Make 2

Figure 1

2. Stitch two C squares to the units from step 1 and join together as shown in Figure 2. Press.

B-C-D Unit
Make 1

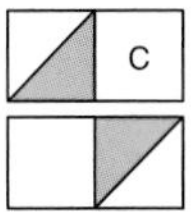

C

Figure 2

3. Stitch one D HST to each side of an A QST as shown in Figure 3. Press. Make 4.

A-D Unit
Make 4

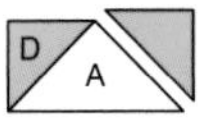

D A

Figure 3

4. Stitch a C square to each end of a unit from step 3 as shown in Figure 4. Press. Make 2.

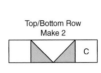
Top/Bottom Row
Make 2

C

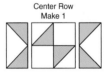
Center Row
Make 1

Figure 4   **Figure 5**

5. Stitch a unit from step 3 to each side of the unit from step 2 as shown in Figure 5. Press.

6. Referring to the photo and Assembly Diagram, lay out all units as shown and stitch together to complete one block. Press.

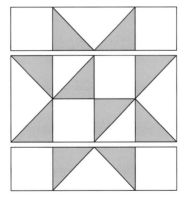

Week No. 31: Butterscotch Star
Assembly Diagram 8½" x 8½"

7. Layer backing right side down, battings and pot holder block right side up. Quilt as desired. Bind pot holder and make hanging loop referring to General Instructions on page 3. ●

Four Corners

Finished Size

Pot Holder Size:
8½" x 8½"

Materials

- 1 (2½" x WOF) coordinating fabric for binding and loop
- Scrap light fabric
- Scrap medium fabric
- Scrap dark fabric
- 10" x 10" backing
- 10" x 10" heat-resistant batting
- 10" x 10" cotton batting
- Thread
- Basic sewing tools and supplies

Project Notes

Read all instructions before beginning this project.

Stitch right sides together using a ¼" seam allowance unless otherwise specified.

Materials and cutting lists assume 40" of usable fabric width for yardage.

WOF – width of fabric
HST – half square triangle ◻
QST – quarter square triangle ⊠

Cutting

From light fabric cut:

- 1 (4⅞") A square then cut once diagonally ◻
- 1 (2⅞") B square then cut once diagonally ◻

From medium fabric cut:

- 1 (4⅞") C square then cut once diagonally ◻
- 1 (2⅞") D square then cut once diagonally ◻

From dark fabric cut:

- 6 (2⅞") E squares then cut once diagonally ◻

Completing the Block

1. Stitch one B HST and one E HST together as shown in Figure 1. Press. Make 2.

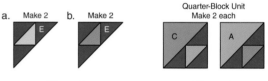

B-E Unit
Make 2

D-E Unit
Make 2

Figure 1   **Figure 2**

2. Stitch one D HST and one E HST together as shown in Figure 2. Press. Make 2.

3. Stitch one E HST to two sides of a unit from step 1 as shown in Figure 3a. Press. Make 2. Stitch one E HST to two sides of unit from step 2 as shown in Figure 3b. Press. Make 2.

a. Make 2   b. Make 2

Quarter-Block Unit
Make 2 each

Figure 3   **Figure 4**

4. Stitch one C HST to a unit from step 3a as shown in Figure 4. Press. Make 2. Stitch one A HST to a unit from step 3b as shown in Figure 4. Press. Make 2.

5. Referring to the photo and Assembly Diagram, lay out all units as shown and stitch together to complete one block. Press.

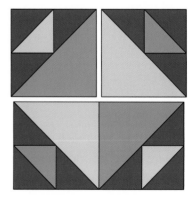

Week No. 32: Four Corners
Assembly Diagram 8½" x 8½"

6. Layer backing right side down, battings and pot holder block right side up. Quilt as desired. Bind pot holder and make hanging loop referring to General Instructions on page 3. ●

Grandma's Vase

Finished Size

Pot Holder Size:
8½" x 8½"

Materials

- 1 (2½" x WOF) coordinating fabric for binding and loop
- Scrap very light fabric
- Scrap light fabric
- Scrap medium fabric
- Scrap dark fabric
- 10" x 10" backing
- 10" x 10" heat-resistant batting
- 10" x 10" cotton batting
- Thread
- Basic sewing tools and supplies

Project Notes

Read all instructions before beginning this project.

Stitch right sides together using a ¼" seam allowance unless otherwise specified.

Materials and cutting lists assume 40" of usable fabric width for yardage.

WOF – width of fabric
HST – half square triangle
QST – quarter square triangle

Cutting

From very light fabric cut:

- 3 (3¼") A squares then cut twice diagonally
- 2 (2⅞") B squares then cut once diagonally

From light fabric cut:

- 1 (4½") C square
- 2 (3¼") D squares then cut twice diagonally

From medium fabric cut:

- 2 (2⅞") E squares then cut once diagonally

From dark fabric cut:

- 3 (3¼") F squares then cut twice diagonally

Completing the Block

1. Stitch one B HST and one E HST together as shown in Figure 1. Press. Make 4.

B-E Unit
Make 4

Figure 1

2. Stitch one A QST and one D QST together as shown in Figure 2a. Press. Make 4. Reversing positions, stitch one A and one D QST together as shown in Figure 2b. Press. Make 4.

A-D Unit
a. Make 4   b. Reversed A-D Unit Make 4

Figure 2

3. Stitch one A QST and one F QST together as shown in Figure 3. Press. Make 4.

A-F Unit
Make 4

Figure 3

4. Stitch one F QST to two sides of the unit from step 3 as shown in Figure 4. Press. Make 4.

Make 4

Figure 4

5. Stitch one unit and one reversed unit from step 2 to each side of the unit from step 4 as shown in Figure 5, confirming placement. Press. Make 4.

Side Unit
Make 4

Figure 5

6. Stitch one unit from step 1 to each end of a unit from step 5 (Figure 6). Press. Make 2.

Top/Bottom Unit
Make 2

Figure 6

7. Referring to the photo and Assembly Diagram, lay out all units and the C piece as shown and stitch together to complete one block. Press.

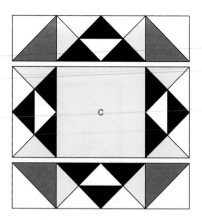

Week No. 33: Grandma's Vase
Assembly Diagram 8½" x 8½"

8. Layer backing right side down, battings and pot holder block right side up. Quilt as desired. Bind pot holder and make hanging loop referring to General Instructions on page 3. ●

Turbines

Finished Size

Pot Holder Size:
8½" x 8½"

Materials

- 1 (2½" x WOF)
  coordinating
  fabric for binding and loop
- Scrap light fabric
- Scrap dark fabric
- 10" x 10" backing
- 10" x 10" heat-resistant batting
- 10" x 10" cotton batting
- Thread
- Basic sewing tools and supplies

Project Notes

Read all instructions before beginning this project.

Stitch right sides together using a ¼" seam allowance unless otherwise specified.

Materials and cutting lists assume 40" of usable fabric width for yardage.

WOF – width of fabric
HST – half square triangle
QST – quarter square triangle ⊠

Cutting

From light fabric cut:

- 4 (2⅞") A squares then cut once diagonally ◺

From dark fabric cut:

- 2 (4⅞") B squares then cut once diagonally ◺
- 4 (2⅞") C squares then cut once diagonally ◺

Completing the Block

1. Stitch one A HST and one C HST together as shown in Figure 1. Press. Make 4.

A-C Unit
Make 4

A-C Unit
Make 4

Figure 1

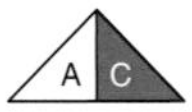

Figure 2

2. Stitch one A HST and one C HST together as shown in Figure 2. Press. Make 4.

3. Stitch the four units from step 1 together to make one unit as shown in Figure 3. Press.

Center Unit
Make 1

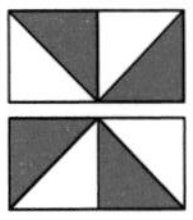

Figure 3

Figure 4

4. Sew two units from step 2 to opposite sides of the unit from step 3 as shown in Figure 4. Press. Sew two units from step 2 to the remaining two sides. Press.

5. Referring to the photo and Assembly Diagram, lay out the unit and B pieces as shown and stitch together to complete one block. Press.

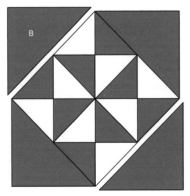

Week No. 34: Turbines
Assembly Diagram 8½" x 8½"

6. Layer backing right side down, battings and pot holder block right side up. Quilt as desired. Bind pot holder and make hanging loop referring to General Instructions on page 3. ●

Grandmother's Favorite

Finished Size

Pot Holder Size:
8½" x 8½"

Materials

- 1 (2½" x WOF) coordinating fabric for binding and loop
- Scrap light fabric
- Scrap dark fabric
- 10" x 10" backing
- 10" x 10" heat-resistant batting
- 10" x 10" cotton batting
- Thread
- Basic sewing tools and supplies

Project Notes

Read all instructions before beginning this project.

Stitch right sides together using a ¼" seam allowance unless otherwise specified.

Materials and cutting lists assume 40" of usable fabric width for yardage.

WOF – width of fabric
HST – half square triangle
QST – quarter square triangle

Cutting

From light fabric cut:

- 1 (4½") A square
- 1 (3¼") B square then cut twice diagonally ⊠
- 6 (2⅞") C squares then cut once diagonally ◻

From dark fabric cut:

- 3 (3¼") D squares then cut twice diagonally ⊠
- 2 (2⅞") E squares then cut once diagonally ◻

Completing the Block

1. Stitch one C HST and one E HST together as shown in Figure 1. Press. Make 4.

C-E Unit
Make 4

Figure 1

2. Stitch one B QST and one D QST together as shown in Figure 2. Press. Make 4.

B-D Unit
Make 4

Figure 2

3. Stitch one D QST to each side of a unit from step 2 as shown in Figure 3. Press. Make 4.

B-D-D Unit
Make 4

Figure 3

4. Stitch one C HST to each side of a unit from step 3 as shown in Figure 4. Press. Make 4.

Side Unit
Make 4

Figure 4

5. Stitch one unit from step 1 to each end of a unit from step 4 as shown in Figure 5. Press. Make 2.

Top/Bottom Unit
Make 2

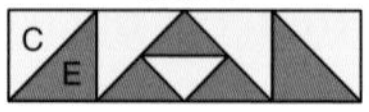

Figure 5

6. Referring to the photo and Assembly Diagram, lay out all units and the A piece as shown and stitch together to complete one block. Press.

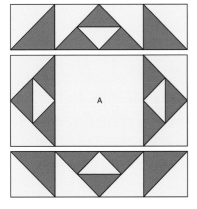

Week No. 35: Grandmother's Favorite
Assembly Diagram 8½" x 8½"

7. Layer backing right side down, battings and pot holder block right side up. Quilt as desired. Bind pot holder and make hanging loop referring to General Instructions on page 3.

Optional Center Square Finish

This is a great block to add a personalized option to. You can add an appliqué to the middle square or stitch a meaningful word, saying or message. In the example given for this block, a simple flower was appliquéd to the center. You'll find several possible appliqué patterns to use throughout this book, or feel free to make your own. Refer to the General Instructions on page 3 for appliqué techniques. ●

Week No. 35 Option: Flower Appliqué
Placement Diagram 8½" x 8½"

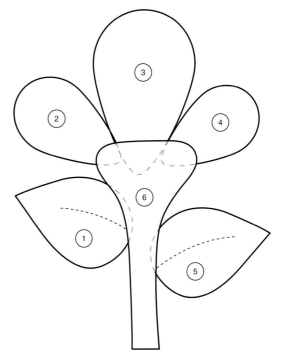

Week No. 35 Option: Grandmother's Favorite
Flower Appliqué

Coffee Shop

Finished Size

Pot Holder Size:
8½" x 8½"

Materials

- 1 (2½" x WOF) coordinating fabric for binding and loop
- Scrap light fabric
- Scrap medium No. 1 fabric
- Scrap medium No. 2 fabric
- Scrap dark fabric
- 10" x 10" backing
- 10" x 10" heat-resistant batting
- 10" x 10" cotton batting
- Thread
- Basic sewing tools and supplies

Project Notes

Read all instructions before beginning this project.

Stitch right sides together using a ¼" seam allowance unless otherwise specified.

Materials and cutting lists assume 40" of usable fabric width for yardage.

WOF – width of fabric
HST – half square triangle ▢
QST – quarter square triangle ▨

Cutting

From light fabric cut:

- 2 (4½") A squares

From medium No. 1 fabric cut:

- 1 (3½") B square

From medium No. 2 fabric cut:

- 1 (3½") B square

From dark fabric cut:

- 4 (1" x 3½") C strips
- 4 (1" x 4½") D strips

Completing the Block

1. Stitch one C strip to opposite sides of a B square as shown in Figure 1. Press. Stitch D strips to the remaining sides. Press. Make 2.

Framed B Unit
Make 2

Figure 1

2. Referring to the photo and Assembly Diagram, lay out both units and A pieces as shown and stitch together to complete one block. Press.

3. Layer backing right side down, battings and pot holder block right side up. Quilt as desired. Bind pot holder and make hanging loop referring to General Instructions on page 3.

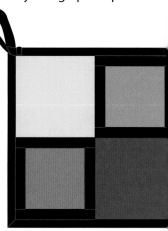

Week No. 36: Coffee Shop
Assembly Diagram 8½" x 8½"

Easy Color Options

This is a great block for quickly using up scraps. Select fabrics from a single color group for the squares and go to town to make several sets to give as gifts. ●

Week No. 36 Option: Alternate Fab
Placement Diagram 8½" x 8½"

Square in a
Square in a Square

Finished Size
Pot Holder Size:
8½" x 8½"

Materials
- 1 (2½" x WOF) coordinating fabric for binding and loop
- Scrap light fabric
- Scrap dark fabric
- 10" x 10" backing
- 10" x 10" heat-resistant batting
- 10" x 10" cotton batting
- Thread
- Basic sewing tools and supplies

Project Notes
Read all instructions before beginning this project.

Stitch right sides together using a ¼" seam allowance unless otherwise specified.

Materials and cutting lists assume 40" of usable fabric width for yardage.

WOF – width of fabric
HST – half square triangle ◻
QST – quarter square triangle ⊠

Cutting

From light fabric cut:
- 1 (5¼") A square then cut twice diagonally ⊠
- 1 (3¼") B squares then cut twice diagonally ⊠

From dark fabric cut:
- 2 (4⅞") C squares then cut once diagonally ◻
- 2 (2⅞") D squares then cut once diagonally ◻
- 1 (2½") E square

Completing the Block

1. Stitch one B QST to opposite sides of the E square as shown in Figure 1. Press.

Figure 1

2. Stitch one B QST to the remaining sides of the unit from step 1 as shown in Figure 2. Press.

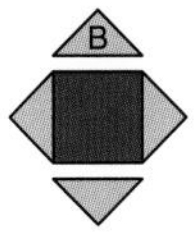

Figure 2

3. Stitch one D HST to opposite sides of the unit from step 2 as shown in Figure 3. Press. Stitch one D HST to the remaining sides. Press.

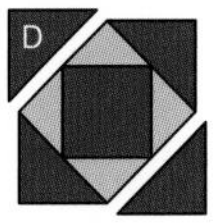

Figure 3

4. Referring to the photo and Assembly Diagram, lay out the unit and pieces as shown and stitch together to complete one block. Press.

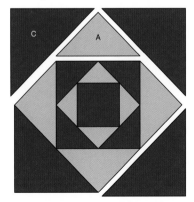

Week No. 37: Square in a Square in a Square
Assembly Diagram 8½" x 8½"

5. Layer backing right side down, battings and pot holder block right side up. Quilt as desired. Bind pot holder and make hanging loop referring to General Instructions on page 3. ●

Ocean Waves

Finished Size
Pot Holder Size:
8½" x 8½"

Materials
- 1 (2½" x WOF) coordinating fabric for binding and loop
- Scrap light fabric
- Scrap medium fabric
- Scrap dark fabric
- 10" x 10" backing
- 10" x 10" heat-resistant batting
- 10" x 10" cotton batting
- Thread
- Basic sewing tools and supplies

Project Notes
Read all instructions before beginning this project.

Stitch right sides together using a ¼" seam allowance unless otherwise specified.

Materials and cutting lists assume 40" of usable fabric width for yardage.

WOF – width of fabric
HST – half square triangle
QST – quarter square triangle ⊠

Cutting
Note: *Cutting instructions will make two blocks.*

From light fabric cut:
- 1 (6⅞") A square then cut once diagonally ◺
- 4 (2⅞") B squares then cut once diagonally ◺

From medium fabric cut:
- 6 (2⅞") C squares then cut once diagonally ◺

From dark fabric cut:
- 1 (6⅞") D square then cut once diagonally ◺
- 4 (2⅞") E squares then cut once diagonally ◺

Completing the Block
1. Stitch one B HST and one E HST together as shown in Figure 1. Press. Make 4.

Figure 1 **Figure 2**

2. Stitch one unit from step 1 and one C HST as shown in Figure 2. Press.

3. Stitch one C HST to each side of a unit from step 1 as shown in Figure 3. Press. Make 2.

Figure 3 **Figure 4**

4. Stitch a C HST to one unit from step 1 as shown in Figure 4. Press.

5. Referring to the photo and Assembly Diagram, lay out all units and pieces as shown and stitch together to complete one block. Press.

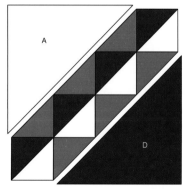

Week No. 38: Ocean Waves
Assembly Diagram 8½" x 8½"

6. Layer backing right side down, battings and pot holder block right side up. Quilt as desired. Bind pot holder and make hanging loop referring to General Instructions on page 3. ●

Puzzle Me

Finished Size

Pot Holder Size:
8½" x 8½"

Materials

- 1 (2½" x WOF) coordinating fabric for binding and loop
- Scrap light fabric
- Scrap medium fabric
- Scrap dark fabric
- 10" x 10" backing
- 10" x 10" heat-resistant batting
- 10" x 10" cotton batting
- Thread
- Basic sewing tools and supplies

Project Notes

Read all instructions before beginning this project.

Stitch right sides together using a ¼" seam allowance unless otherwise specified.

Materials and cutting lists assume 40" of usable fabric width for yardage.

WOF – width of fabric
HST – half square triangle ◻
QST – quarter square triangle ⊠

Cutting

From light fabric cut:

- 1 (2½" x 6½") A rectangle
- 1 (2½" x 4½") B rectangle
- 1 (2½") C square

From medium fabric cut:

- 4 (2½") D squares

From dark fabric cut:

- 1 (2½" x 6½") E rectangle
- 1 (2½" x 4½") F rectangle
- 1 (2½") G square

Completing the Block

1. Referring to Figure 1, stitch one G and one D square together. Press. Stitch one D and one C square together. Press. Stitch rows together to make a unit. Press.

Four-Patch Unit
Make 1

Figure 1

2. Stitch one B and one F rectangle to opposite sides of the unit from step 1 as shown in Figure 2. Press.

Center Unit
Make 1

D-E Unit
Make 1

A-D Unit
Make 1

Figure 2   **Figure 3**

3. Stitch one D square to an E rectangle and a D square to an A rectangle as shown in Figure 3. Press.

4. Referring to the photo and Assembly Diagram, lay out all units as shown and stitch together to complete one block. Press.

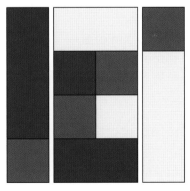

Week No. 39: Puzzle Me
Assembly Diagram 8½" x 8½"

5. Layer backing right side down, battings and pot holder block right side up. Quilt as desired. Bind pot holder and make hanging loop referring to General Instructions on page 3. ●

King's Crown

Finished Size

Pot Holder Size:
8½" x 8½"

Materials

- 1 (2½" x WOF) coordinating fabric for binding and loop
- Scrap light fabric
- Scrap dark No. 1 fabric
- Scrap dark No. 2 fabric
- 10" x 10" backing
- 10" x 10" heat-resistant batting
- 10" x 10" cotton batting
- Thread
- Basic sewing tools and supplies

Project Notes

Read all instructions before beginning this project.

Stitch right sides together using a ¼" seam allowance unless otherwise specified.

Materials and cutting lists assume 40" of usable fabric width for yardage.

WOF – width of fabric
HST – half square triangle
QST – quarter square triangle ⊠

Cutting

From light fabric cut:

- 1 (4½") A square
- 4 (2⅞") B squares then cut once diagonally ◻

From dark No. 1 fabric cut:

- 4 (2¼") C squares

From dark No. 2 fabric cut:

- 1 (5¼") D square then cut twice diagonally ⊠

Completing the Block

1. Stitch one B HST to opposite sides of a D QST as shown in Figure 1. Press. Make 4.

B-D Unit
Make 4

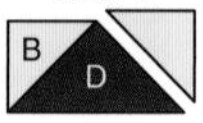

Figure 1

2. Stitch one C square to each end of one unit from step 1 as shown in Figure 2. Press. Make 2.

Top/Bottom Row
Make 2

Figure 2

3. Stitch one unit from step 1 to each side of an A square as shown in Figure 3. Press.

Center Row
Make 1

Figure 3

4. Referring to the photo and Assembly Diagram, lay out all units as shown and stitch together to complete one block. Press.

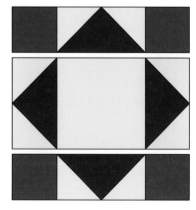

Week No. 40: King's Crown
Assembly Diagram 8½" x 8½"

5. Layer backing right side down, battings and pot holder block right side up. Quilt as desired. Bind pot holder and make hanging loop referring to General Instructions on page 3.

Optional Fussy-Cut Center Square

This is a great block for utilizing focal fabrics. Use a fussy-cut motif for the center square to complement a kitchen theme or colors. In the example given for these blocks, motifs were fussy-cut from a fabric featuring different birds. Refer to the General Instructions on page 3 for fussy-cutting techniques. ●

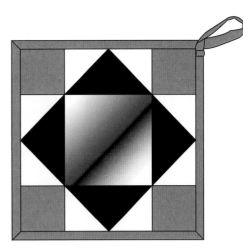

Week No. 40 Option 2: Fussy-Cut Center
Placement Diagram 8½" x 8½"

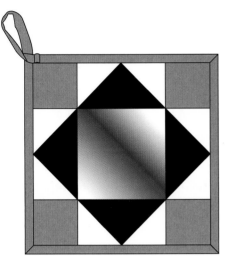

Week No. 40 Option 1: Fussy-Cut Center
Placement Diagram 8½" x 8½"

Magic Triangles

Finished Size

Pot Holder Size:
8½" x 8½"

Materials

- 1 (2½" x WOF)
coordinating
fabric for binding and loop
- Scrap light fabric
- Scrap medium No. 1 fabric
- Scrap medium No. 2 fabric
- Scrap dark fabric
- 10" x 10" backing
- 10" x 10" heat-resistant batting
- 10" x 10" cotton batting
- Thread
- Basic sewing tools and supplies

Project Notes

Read all instructions before beginning this project.

Stitch right sides together using a ¼" seam allowance unless otherwise specified.

Materials and cutting lists assume 40" of usable fabric width for yardage.

WOF – width of fabric
HST – half square triangle
QST – quarter square triangle ⊠

Cutting

From light fabric cut:

- 8 (2⅞") A squares then cut once diagonally ◻

From medium No. 1 fabric cut:

- 1 (2⅞") B square then cut once diagonally ◻

From medium No. 2 fabric cut:

- 1 (2⅞") C square then cut once diagonally ◻

From dark fabric cut:

- 1 (5¼") D square then cut twice diagonally ⊠
- 2 (2⅞") E squares then cut once diagonally ◻

Completing the Block

1. Stitch one A HST to each side of a D QST as shown in Figure 1. Press. Make 4.

Figure 1　　　**Figure 2**

2. Stitch one A HST and one B HST together as shown in Figure 2a. Press. Stitch one A HST and one C HST together as shown in Figure 2b. Press. Make 2 each.

3. Stitch the units from step 2 together as shown in Figure 3. Press.

Figure 3　　　**Figure 4**

4. Stitch one A HST and one E HST together as shown in Figure 4. Press. Make 4.

5. Stitch one unit from step 4 to each end of a unit from step 1 as shown in Figure 5. Press. Make 2.

Figure 5

6. Referring to the photo and Assembly Diagram, lay out all units as shown and stitch together to complete one block. Press.

7. Layer backing right side down, battings and pot holder block right side up. Quilt as desired. Bind pot holder and make hanging loop referring to General Instructions on page 3. ●

Week No. 41: Magic Triangles
Assembly Diagram 8½" x 8½"

Sunny-Side Up

Finished Size

Pot Holder Size:
8½" x 8½"

Materials

- 1 (2½" x WOF)
  coordinating
  fabric for binding and loop
- Scrap light fabric
- Scrap dark fabric
- 10" x 10" backing
- 10" x 10" heat-resistant batting
- 10" x 10" cotton batting
- Thread
- Basic sewing tools and supplies

Project Notes

Read all instructions before beginning this project.

Stitch right sides together using a ¼" seam allowance unless otherwise specified.

Materials and cutting lists assume 40" of usable fabric width for yardage.

WOF – width of fabric
HST – half square triangle
QST – quarter square triangle

Cutting

From light fabric cut:

- 6 (2⅞") A square then cut once diagonally
- 4 (2½") B squares

From dark fabric cut:

- 6 (2⅞") C squares then cut once diagonally

Completing the Block

1. Stitch one A HST and one C HST together as shown in Figure 1. Press. Make 12.

A-C Unit
Make 12

Figure 1

2. Stitch two units from step 1 together as shown in Figure 2. Press. Make 4.

Make 4

Figure 2

3. Stitch one B square to a unit from step 1 as shown in Figure 3. Press. Make 4.

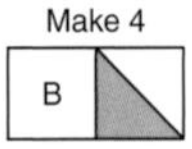

Make 4

Figure 3

4. Referring to the photo and Assembly Diagram, lay out all units as shown and stitch together to complete one block. Press.

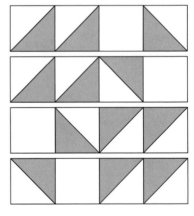

Week No. 42: Sunny-Side Up
Assembly Diagram 8½" x 8½"

5. Layer backing right side down, battings and pot holder block right side up. Quilt as desired. Bind pot holder and make hanging loop referring to General Instructions on page 3. ●

Autumn Star

Finished Size

Pot Holder Size: 8½" x 8½"

Materials

- 1 (2½" x WOF) coordinating fabric for binding and loop
- Scrap light fabric
- Scrap medium fabric
- Scrap dark fabric
- 10" x 10" backing
- 10" x 10" heat-resistant batting
- 10" x 10" cotton batting
- Thread
- Basic sewing tools and supplies

Project Notes

Read all instructions before beginning this project.

Stitch right sides together using a ¼" seam allowance unless otherwise specified.

Materials and cutting lists assume 40" of usable fabric width for yardage.

WOF – width of fabric
HST – half square triangle ◻
QST – quarter square triangle ⊠

Cutting

From light fabric cut:

- 1 (5¼") A square then cut twice diagonally ⊠
- 2 (2⅞") B squares then cut once diagonally ◻
- 1 (3⅜") C squares

From medium fabric cut:

- 1 (5¼") D square then cut twice diagonally ⊠
- 2 (2⅞") E squares then cut once diagonally ◻

From dark fabric cut:

- 2 (2⅞") F squares then cut once diagonally ◻

Completing the Block

1. Stitch one B HST and one E HST together as shown in Figure 1. Press. Make 4.

B-E Unit
Make 4

Figure 1

2. Stitch one unit from step 1 and one D QST as shown in Figure 2. Press. Make 4.

B-D-E Unit
Make 4

Figure 2

3. Stitch one F HST to each unit from step 2 as shown in Figure 3. Press. Make 4.

Corner Unit
Make 4

Figure 3

4. Referring to the photo and Assembly Diagram, lay out all units and pieces as shown and stitch together to complete one block. Press.

5. Layer backing right side down, battings and pot holder block right side up. Quilt as desired. Bind pot holder and make hanging loop referring to General Instructions on page 3. ●

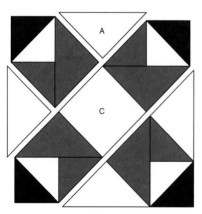

Week No. 43: Autumn Star
Assembly Diagram 8½" x 8½"

Fly Away Home

Finished Size

Pot Holder Size:
8½" x 8½"

Materials

- 1 (2½" x WOF) coordinating fabric for binding and loop
- Scrap light fabric
- Scrap medium fabric
- Scrap dark fabric
- 10" x 10" backing
- 10" x 10" heat-resistant batting
- 10" x 10" cotton batting
- Thread
- Basic sewing tools and supplies

Project Notes

Read all instructions before beginning this project.

Stitch right sides together using a ¼" seam allowance unless otherwise specified.

Materials and cutting lists assume 40" of usable fabric width for yardage.

WOF – width of fabric
HST – half square triangle
QST – quarter square triangle

Cutting

From light fabric cut:

- 1 (4⅞") A square then cut once diagonally

From medium fabric cut:

- 1 (4⅞") B square then cut once diagonally

From dark fabric cut:

- 2 (4½") C squares

Completing the Block

1. Stitch one A HST and one B HST together as shown in Figure 1. Press. Make 2.

A-B Unit
Make 2

A
B

Figure 1

2. Referring to the photo and Assembly Diagram, lay out both units and C pieces as shown and stitch together to complete one block. Press.

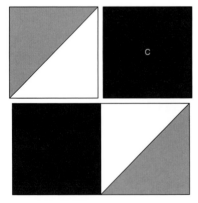

C

Week No. 44: Fly Away Home
Assembly Diagram 8½" x 8½"

3. Layer backing right side down, battings and pot holder block right side up. Quilt as desired. Bind pot holder and make hanging loop referring to General Instructions on page 3. ●

Picture Perfect

Finished Size

Pot Holder Size:
8½" x 8½"

Materials

- 1 (2½" x WOF) coordinating fabric for binding and loop
- Scrap light fabric
- Scrap dark fabric
- 10" x 10" backing
- 10" x 10" heat-resistant batting
- 10" x 10" cotton batting
- Thread
- Basic sewing tools and supplies

Project Notes

Read all instructions before beginning this project.

Stitch right sides together using a ¼" seam allowance unless otherwise specified.

Materials and cutting lists assume 40" of usable fabric width for yardage.

WOF – width of fabric
HST – half square triangle
QST – quarter square triangle

Cutting

From light fabric cut:

- 2 (2⅞") A squares then cut once diagonally
- 4 (2½") B squares

From dark fabric cut:

- 4 (2½" x 4½") C rectangles
- 1 (3⅜") D square

Completing the Block

1. Stitch one A HST to opposites sides of the D square as shown in Figure 1. Press. Stitch one A HST to the remaining sides. Press.

A-D Unit
Make 1

Figure 1

2. Stitch B squares to each end of a C rectangle as shown in Figure 2. Press. Make 2.

Top/Bottom Row
Make 2

Figure 2

3. Stitch one C rectangle to opposites sides of the unit from step 1 as shown in Figure 3. Press.

Center Row
Make 1

Figure 3

4. Referring to the photo and Assembly Diagram, lay out all units as shown and stitch together to complete one block. Press.

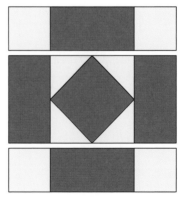

Week No. 45: Picture Perfect
Assembly Diagram 8½" x 8½"

5. Layer backing right side down, battings and pot holder block right side up. Quilt as desired. Bind pot holder and make hanging loop referring to General Instructions on page 3.

Optional Center Square Finish

This is a great block to add a personalized option to. You can add an appliqué to the middle block or stitch in a meaningful word, saying or message. In the example given for this block, a cute fish was appliquéd to the center. You'll find several possible appliqué patterns to use throughout this book, or feel free to make your own. Refer to the General Instructions on page 3 for appliqué techniques. ●

Week No. 45 Option: Fish Appliqué
Placement Diagram 8½" x 8½"

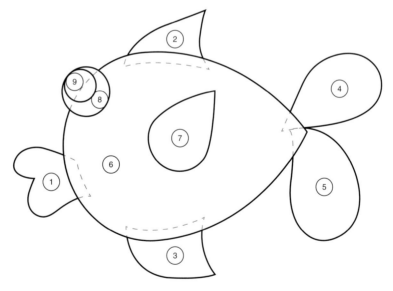

Week No. 45 Option: Picture Perfect
Fish Appliqué

Louisiana

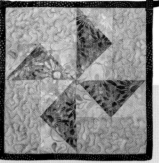

Finished Size

Pot Holder Size:
8½" x 8½"

Materials

- 1 (2½" x WOF)
  coordinating
  fabric for binding and loop
- Scrap light fabric
- Scrap medium fabric
- Scrap dark fabric
- 10" x 10" backing
- 10" x 10" heat-resistant batting
- 10" x 10" cotton batting
- Thread
- Basic sewing tools and supplies

Project Notes

Read all instructions before beginning this project.

Stitch right sides together using a ¼" seam allowance unless otherwise specified.

Materials and cutting lists assume 40" of usable fabric width for yardage.

WOF – width of fabric
HST – half square triangle
QST – quarter square triangle

Cutting

From light fabric cut:

- 4 (2½" x 4½") A rectangles

From medium fabric cut:

- 4 (2⅞") B squares then cut once diagonally

From dark fabric cut:

- 1 (5¼") C square then cut twice diagonally

Completing the Block

1. Stitch one B HST to each side of a C QST as shown in Figure 1. Press. Make 4.

B-C Unit
Make 4

Figure 1

2. Stitch one unit from step 1 and one A rectangle together as shown in Figure 2. Press. Make 4.

Quarter Block Unit
Make 4

Figure 2

3. Referring to the photo and Assembly Diagram, lay out all units as shown and stitch together to complete one block. Press.

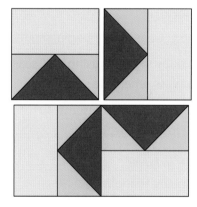

Week No. 46: Louisiana
Assembly Diagram 8½" x 8½"

4. Layer backing right side down, battings and pot holder block right side up. Quilt as desired. Bind pot holder and make hanging loop referring to General Instructions on page 3. ●

Uneven Nine-Patch

Finished Size

Pot Holder Size:
8½" x 8½"

Materials

- 1 (2½" x WOF) coordinating fabric for binding and loop
- Scrap light fabric
- Scrap dark fabric
- 10" x 10" backing
- 10" x 10" heat-resistant batting
- 10" x 10" cotton batting
- Thread
- Basic sewing tools and supplies

Project Notes

Read all instructions before beginning this project.

Stitch right sides together using a ¼" seam allowance unless otherwise specified.

Materials and cutting lists assume 40" of usable fabric width for yardage.

WOF – width of fabric
HST – half square triangle ◻
QST – quarter square triangle ⊠

Cutting

From light fabric cut:

- 4 (2½" x 4½") A rectangles

From dark fabric cut:

- 1 (4½") B square
- 4 (2½") C squares

Completing the Block

1. Stitch one C square to each end of an A rectangle as shown in Figure 1. Press. Make 2.

Top/Bottom Row
Make 2

Figure 1

2. Stitch one A rectangle on opposite sides of the B square as shown in Figure 2. Press.

Center Row
Make 1

Figure 2

3. Referring to the photo and Assembly Diagram, lay out all units as shown and stitch together to complete one block. Press.

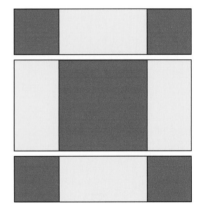

Week No. 47: Uneven Nine-Patch
Assembly Diagram 8½" x 8½"

4. Layer backing right side down, battings and pot holder block right side up. Quilt as desired. Bind pot holder and make hanging loop referring to General Instructions on page 3.

Optional Center Square Finish

This is a great block to add a personalized option to. You can add an appliqué to the middle square or stitch in a meaningful word, saying or message. In the example given for this block, a holly motif was appliquéd to the center for a festive holiday feel. You'll find several possible appliqué patterns to use throughout this book, or feel free to make your own. Refer to the General Instructions on page 3 for appliqué techniques. ●

Week No. 47 Option: Holly Appliqué
Placement Diagram 8¹⁄₂" x 8¹⁄₂"

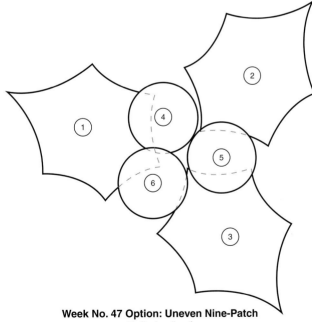

Week No. 47 Option: Uneven Nine-Patch
Holly Appliqué

Tropical Island

Finished Size

Pot Holder Size:
8½" x 8½"

Materials

- 1 (2½" x WOF) coordinating fabric for binding and loop
- Scrap light fabric
- Scrap dark fabric
- 10" x 10" backing
- 10" x 10" heat-resistant batting
- 10" x 10" cotton batting
- Thread
- Basic sewing tools and supplies

Project Notes

Read all instructions before beginning this project.

Stitch right sides together using a ¼" seam allowance unless otherwise specified.

Materials and cutting lists assume 40" of usable fabric width for yardage.

WOF – width of fabric
HST – half square triangle
QST – quarter square triangle

Cutting

From light fabric cut:

- 1 (5¼") A square then cut twice diagonally
- 2 (2⅞") B squares then cut once diagonally
- 1 (3⅜") C square

From dark fabric cut:

- 4 (3⅜") D squares

Completing the Block

1. Stitch one A QST to opposite sides of a D square as shown in Figure 1. Press. Make 2.

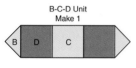

A-D Unit
Make 2

Figure 1

2. Stitch B HST and D squares to opposite sides of the C square as shown in Figure 2. Press.

B-C-D Unit
Make 1

Figure 2

3. Referring to the photo and Assembly Diagram, lay out all units as shown and stitch together to complete one block. Press.

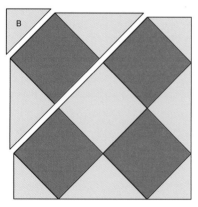

Week No. 48: Tropical Island
Assembly Diagram 8½" x 8½"

4. Layer backing right side down, battings and pot holder block right side up. Quilt as desired. Bind pot holder and make hanging loop referring to General Instructions on page 3. ●

Sawtooth Star

Finished Size

Pot Holder Size:
8½" x 8½"

Materials

- 1 (2½" x WOF)
  coordinating
  fabric for binding and loop
- Scrap light fabric
- Scrap medium fabric
- Scrap dark fabric
- 10" x 10" backing
- 10" x 10" heat-resistant batting
- 10" x 10" cotton batting
- Thread
- Basic sewing tools and supplies

Project Notes

Read all instructions before beginning this project.

Stitch right sides together using a ¼" seam allowance unless otherwise specified.

Materials and cutting lists assume 40" of usable fabric width for yardage.

WOF – width of fabric
HST – half square triangle ◻
QST – quarter square triangle ⊠

Cutting

From light fabric cut:

- 1 (5¼") A square then cut twice diagonally ⊠
- 4 (2½") B squares

From medium fabric cut:

- 1 (4½") C square

From dark fabric cut:

- 4 (2⅞") D squares then cut once diagonally ◻

Completing the Block

1. Stitch one D HST to each side of an A QST as shown in Figure 1. Press. Make 4.

A-D Unit
Make 4

Figure 1

2. Stitch one B square to each end of a unit from step 1 as shown in Figure 2. Press. Make 2.

Top/Bottom Row
Make 2

Figure 2

3. Stitch one unit from step 1 to opposite sides of the C square as shown in Figure 3. Press.

Center Row
Make 1

Figure 3

4. Referring to the photo and Assembly Diagram, lay out all units as shown and stitch together to complete one block. Press.

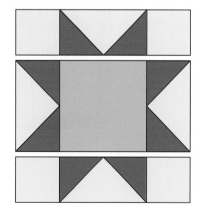

Week No. 49: Sawtooth Star
Assembly Diagram 8½" x 8½"

5. Layer backing right side down, battings and pot holder block right side up. Quilt as desired. Bind pot holder and make hanging loop referring to General Instructions on page 3.

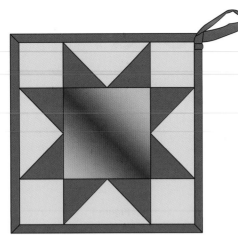

Week No. 49 Option: Fussy-Cut Center
Placement Diagram 8½" x 8½"

Optional Fussy-Cut Center Square

This is a great block for utilizing focal fabrics. Use a fussy-cut motif for the center square to complement a kitchen theme or colors. In the example given for this block, a fun fabric was fussy-cut to feature a figure playing a horn. Refer to the General Instructions on page 3 for fussy-cutting techniques. ●

The Wheel Goes Round

Finished Size

Pot Holder
Size: 8½" x 8½"

Materials

- 1 (2½" x WOF) coordinating fabric for binding and loop
- Scrap light fabric
- Scrap dark fabric
- 10" x 10" backing
- 10" x 10" heat-resistant batting
- 10" x 10" cotton batting
- Thread
- Basic sewing tools and supplies

Project Notes

Read all instructions before beginning this project.

Stitch right sides together using a ¼" seam allowance unless otherwise specified.

Materials and cutting lists assume 40" of usable fabric width for yardage.

WOF – width of fabric
HST – half square triangle ◳
QST – quarter square triangle ⊠

Cutting

From light fabric cut:

- 2 (5¼") A squares then cut twice diagonally ⊠
- 2 (2⅞") B squares then cut once diagonally ◳

From dark fabric cut:

- 1 (5¼") C square then cut twice diagonally ⊠
- 1 (3⅜") D square

Completing the Block

1. Stitch one A QST and one C QST together as shown in Figure 1. Press. Make 4.

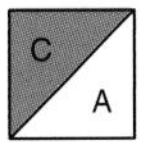

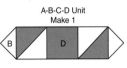

A-C Unit Make 4

A-A-C Unit Make 2

Figure 1 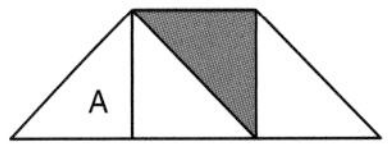   **Figure 2**

2. Stitch one A QST to opposite sides of a unit from step 1 as shown in Figure 2. Press. Make 2.

3. Stitch one B HST and one unit from step 1 to opposite sides of a D square as shown in Figure 3. Press.

A-B-C-D Unit Make 1

Figure 3

4. Referring to the photo and Assembly Diagram, lay out all units and the remaining B pieces as shown and stitch together to complete one block. Press.

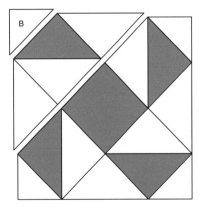

Week No. 50: The Wheel Goes Round
Assembly Diagram 8½" x 8½"

5. Layer backing right side down, battings and pot holder block right side up. Quilt as desired. Bind pot holder and make hanging loop referring to General Instructions on page 3. ●

Envelopes

Finished Size

Pot Holder Size:
8½" x 8½"

Materials

- 1 (2½" x WOF) coordinating fabric for binding and loop
- Scrap light fabric
- Scrap dark fabric
- 10" x 10" backing
- 10" x 10" heat-resistant batting
- 10" x 10" cotton batting
- Thread
- Basic sewing tools and supplies

Project Notes

Read all instructions before beginning this project.

Stitch right sides together using a ¼" seam allowance unless otherwise specified.

Materials and cutting lists assume 40" of usable fabric width for yardage.

WOF – width of fabric
HST – half square triangle ◻
QST – quarter square triangle ⊠

Cutting

From light fabric cut:

- 1 (5¼") A square then cut twice diagonally ⊠
- 2 (2⅞") B squares then cut once diagonally ◻
- 1 (3⅜") C square

From dark fabric cut:

- 1 (5¼") D square then cut twice diagonally ⊠
- 4 (2⅞") E squares then cut once diagonally ◻

Completing the Block

1. Stitch one B HST and one E HST together as shown in Figure 1a. Press. Reversing positions, stitch one B and one E HST together as shown in Figure 1b. Press. Make 2 each.

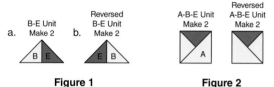

Figure 1   **Figure 2**

2. Stitch an A QST to each unit from step 1 as shown in Figure 2. Press. Make 2 each.

3. Stitch one E HST to each unit from step 2 as shown in Figure 3. Press. Make 2 each.

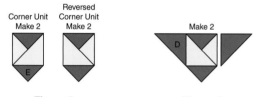

Figure 3   **Figure 4**

4. Stitch one D QST to opposite sides of a reversed corner unit from step 3 as shown in Figure 4. Press. Make 2.

5. Referring to the photo and Assembly Diagram, lay out all units and C piece as shown and stitch together to complete one block. Press.

6. Layer backing right side down, battings and pot holder block right side up. Quilt as desired. Bind pot holder and make hanging loop referring to General Instructions on page 3. ●

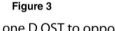

Week No. 51: Envelopes
Assembly Diagram 8½" x 8½"

Bird's-Eye View

Finished Size

Pot Holder Size:
8½" x 8½"

Materials

- 1 (2½" x WOF) coordinating fabric for binding and loop
- Scrap light fabric
- Scrap dark fabric
- 10" x 10" backing
- 10" x 10" heat-resistant batting
- 10" x 10" cotton batting
- Thread
- Basic sewing tools and supplies

Project Notes

Read all instructions before beginning this project.

Stitch right sides together using a ¼" seam allowance unless otherwise specified.

Materials and cutting lists assume 40" of usable fabric width for yardage.

WOF – width of fabric
HST – half square triangle
QST – quarter square triangle

Cutting

From light fabric cut:

- 6 (2⅞") A squares then cut once diagonally
- 1 (3⅜") B square

From dark fabric cut:

- 1 (5¼") C square then cut twice diagonally
- 4 (2⅞") D squares then cut once diagonally

Completing the Block

1. Stitch one A HST and one D HST together as shown in Figure 1. Press. Make 4.

A-D Unit
Make 4

Figure 1

2. Stitch one A HST to each side of a C QST as shown in Figure 2. Press. Make 4.

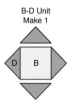

A-C Unit
Make 4

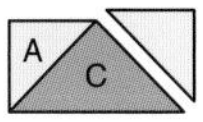

Figure 2

3. Stitch one D HST to opposite sides of a B square as shown in Figure 3. Press. Stitch one D HST to the remaining sides. Press.

B-D Unit
Make 1

Figure 3

4. Referring to the photo and Assembly Diagram, lay out all units as shown and stitch together to complete one block. Press.

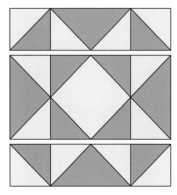

Week No. 52: Bird's-Eye View
Assembly Diagram 8½" x 8½"

5. Layer backing right side down, battings and pot holder block right side up. Quilt as desired. Bind pot holder and make hanging loop referring to General Instructions on page 3. ●

Quilting Basics

The following is a reference guide. For more information, consult a comprehensive quilting book.

Quilt Backing & Batting

We suggest that you cut your backing and batting 8" larger than the finished quilt-top size. If preparing the backing from standard-width fabrics, remove the selvages and sew two or three lengths together; press seams open. If using 108"-wide fabric, trim to size on the straight grain of the fabric.

Prepare batting the same size as your backing. You can purchase prepackaged sizes or battings by the yard and trim to size.

Quilting

1. Press quilt top on both sides and trim all loose threads.
2. Make a quilt sandwich by layering the backing right side down, batting and quilt top centered right side up on flat surface and smooth out. Pin or baste layers together to hold.
3. Mark quilting design on quilt top and quilt as desired by hand or machine. ***Note:*** *If you are sending your quilt to a professional quilter, contact them for specifics about preparing your quilt for quilting.*
4. When quilting is complete, remove pins or basting. Trim batting and backing edges even with raw edges of quilt top.

Binding the Quilt

1. Join binding strips on short ends with diagonal seams to make one long strip; trim seams to ¼" and press seams open (Figure A).

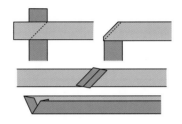

Figure A

2. Fold 1" of one short end to wrong side and press. Fold the binding strip in half with wrong sides together along length, again referring to Figure A; press.
3. Starting about 3" from the folded short end, sew binding to quilt top edges, matching raw edges and using a ¼" seam. Stop stitching ¼" from corner and backstitch (Figure B).

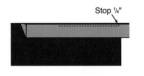

Stop ¼"

Figure B

4. Fold binding up at a 45-degree angle to seam and then down even with quilt edges, forming a pleat at corner, referring to Figure C.

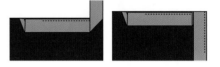

Figure C

5. Resume stitching from corner edge as shown in Figure C, down quilt side, backstitching ¼" from next corner. Repeat, mitering all corners, stitching to within 3" of starting point.
6. Trim binding end long enough to tuck inside starting end and complete stitching (Figure D).

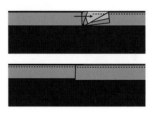

Figure D

7. Fold binding to quilt back and stitch in place by hand or machine to complete your quilt.

Project Gallery

Week 1:
Anvil, 10

Week 2:
Devil's Claw, 11

Week 3:
In Flight, 12

Week 4:
Cypress, 13

Week 4:
Option, 13

Week 5:
Doubles, 15

Week 6:
Cross to Bear, 16

Week 6:
Option, 16

Week 7:
Bailey's Block, 17

Week 8:
Yin Yang, 18

Week 9:
Connecticut, 19

Week 10:
Fortress, 20

Week 11:
Square in a
Square, 21

Week 11:
Option, 21

Week 12:
Dutchman's
Puzzle, 23

Week 13:
Square Me Up, 24

Week 13:
Option, 24

Week 14:
Double X, 26

Week 14:
Option, 26

Week 15:
Electric Fan, 28

Week 16:
Bow Ties &
Checks, 29

Week 17:
Crystal Star, 30

Week 18:
Crosses &
Losses, 31

Week 19:
Cross in a
Square, 32

Week 20:
Diana's Dart, 33

Week 21:
Rotating Star, 34

Week 22:
Economy Block, 35

Week 23:
Double Four-
Patch, 36

Week 24:
This Way
Home, 37

Week 24:
Option, 37

Week 25:
My Flower
Basket, 40

Week 25:
Option, 40

Week 26:
Triangle Affair, 42

Week 27:
Moon Glow, 43

Week 28:
Fair & Square, 44

Week 29:
Ollie's Square, 45

Project Gallery

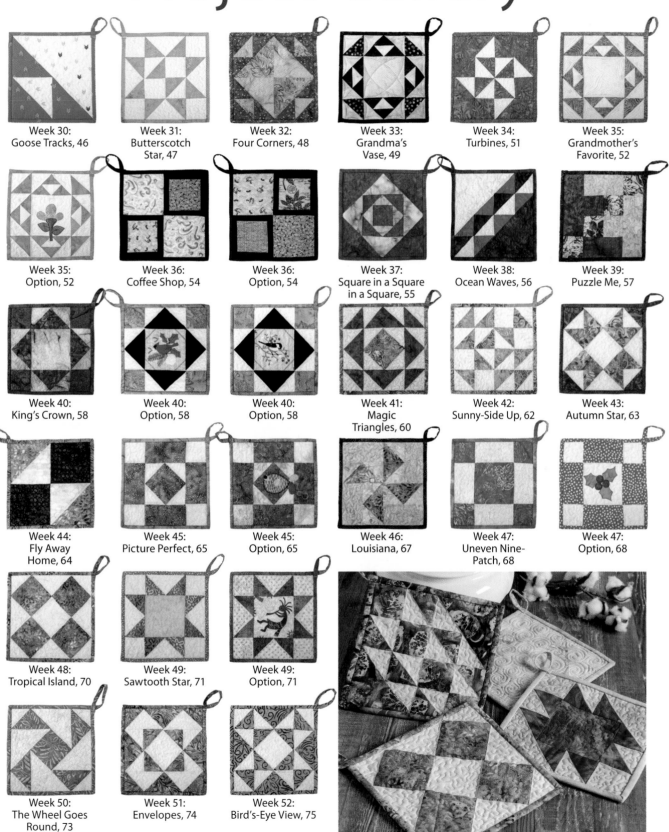

Week 30:
Goose Tracks, 46

Week 31:
Butterscotch
Star, 47

Week 32:
Four Corners, 48

Week 33:
Grandma's
Vase, 49

Week 34:
Turbines, 51

Week 35:
Grandmother's
Favorite, 52

Week 35:
Option, 52

Week 36:
Coffee Shop, 54

Week 36:
Option, 54

Week 37:
Square in a Square
in a Square, 55

Week 38:
Ocean Waves, 56

Week 39:
Puzzle Me, 57

Week 40:
King's Crown, 58

Week 40:
Option, 58

Week 40:
Option, 58

Week 41:
Magic
Triangles, 60

Week 42:
Sunny-Side Up, 62

Week 43:
Autumn Star, 63

Week 44:
Fly Away
Home, 64

Week 45:
Picture Perfect, 65

Week 45:
Option, 65

Week 46:
Louisiana, 67

Week 47:
Uneven Nine-
Patch, 68

Week 47:
Option, 68

Week 48:
Tropical Island, 70

Week 49:
Sawtooth Star, 71

Week 49:
Option, 71

Week 50:
The Wheel Goes
Round, 73

Week 51:
Envelopes, 74

Week 52:
Bird's-Eye View, 75

Supplies

We would like to thank the following manufacturers who provided materials to our designer to make sample projects for this book.

Fabrics for this book were generously donated by the following textile companies:

Hoffman California-International Fabrics

Moda Fabrics

Northcott Fabrics

All battings, fusible webs and stabilizers were generously donated by Bosal:

Katahdin Premium 100 percent cotton batting

Poly-Therm #364B heat-reflective fleece

Fashion-Fuse #300 woven fusible stabilizer

Splendid Web #345 fusible web with paper release

Annie's® Published by Annie's, 306 East Parr Road, Berne, IN 46711. Printed in USA. Copyright © 2019, 2020 Annie's. All rights reserved. This publication may not be reproduced in part or in whole without written permission from the publisher.

RETAIL STORES: If you would like to carry this publication or any other Annie's publications, visit AnniesWSL.com.

Every effort has been made to ensure that the instructions in this publication are complete and accurate. We cannot, however, take responsibility for human error, typographical mistakes or variations in individual work. Please visit AnniesCustomerService.com to check for pattern updates.

ISBN: 978-1-64025-062-8

456789

Introduction

Year of Pot Holders 2 is not only a collection of great pot holders, but also the opportunity to learn and make 8" finished blocks that can be used to design your own quilt projects. These skill-building blocks are just what you need to inspire you to learn new and exciting ideas, and to encourage you to take the next step.

Explore the many possibilities for creating fun pot holders as gifts for those you care about and gain the ability to add those special elements, such as quilted messages and appliqués, to make them unique. Sometimes a small project is just what you need. In a free afternoon, you can finish an easy-but-meaningful project in just an hour or two, and you'll be able to personalize it with easy techniques and a bit of imagination.

For the purpose of a pot holder, the 8½" unfinished blocks in this book work perfectly. But don't stop there! Use these blocks to make table runners, toppers, wall hangings, and lot and lots of quilts. The possibilities are endless. This is your opportunity to design your own projects. Go ahead and take the next step!

Enjoy!

Meet the Designer

Carolyn S. Vagts is a wife, mother, grandmother, quilt designer, author, quilt book editor and editor of *Quilter's World* magazine. She also has owned a successful quilt shop.

Carolyn has made a name for herself in the quilting community with her award-winning techniques of mixing traditional piecing with fusible art appliqué. She especially likes to teach beginner quilt classes, wanting every student to have a good first experience with quilting. She also lectures and teaches workshops throughout the country to guilds.

Table of Contents